I0557279

CLACKAMAS LITERARY REVIEW

2013
Volume XVII

Clackamas Community College
Oregon City, Oregon

CLR
CLACKAMAS LITERARY REVIEW

Editor in Chief
Ryan Davis

Associate Editors
Trevor Dodge
Cosette LeMay
Matthew Warren

Assistant Editors
Rianna Cline Sara Ellington
Sheridan Gately Dylan Plotner

Cover Art
Bri'Anne Parkin
"la Petite Venise"

Journal Design
Matthew Warren

The Clackamas Literary Review is published annually at Clackamas Community College. Manuscripts are read from September 1st to January 31st and will not be returned. By submitting your work to *CLR*, you indicate your consent for us to publish that work in print and online. This issue is $10; issues I–XI are $6 if ordered through *CLR*; issues XII–XVI are available through your favorite online bookseller.

Clackamas Literary Review
19600 Molalla Avenue, Oregon City, Oregon 97045
ISBN: 978-0-9796882-5-6
Printed by Lightning Source
www.clackamasliteraryreview.org

CONTENTS

Editor in Chief's Note

Clackamas Literary Review, like every home for literature, is and should be expansive. All writers can find room to stretch out, unpack, laze about, and be comfortable. The table we set has a place for everyone. Two Clackamas Community College students sit next to Oregon's Poet Laureate, and they share a conversation with professors, housewives, lawyers, playwrights, artists, editors, custodians, musicians, rabbis, and more. The words they share allow us all to become more than we were. Their words move us toward something better—something we can all be proud of. We can sit next to the fire they've made and warm ourselves. Stay as long as you want—there's plenty of room.

Dream big,
Ryan Davis
Editor in Chief

Vivarium

Richard King Perkins II

You have a penchant for subdued arrivals
so events are already beginning.

The scrawl of corona expects erasing
sometime in the evening.
She will not be disappointed.

Fallen leaves dampen further,
mute and benumbed,
though their indulgence in abstraction
will not bring them back to life.

The stain of mulberries
renounces a scattering of earth
while rabbits return to the clasp
of their subterranean utopia.

Superstition invents a thousand tales
about this very night
though there is no story here worth telling.

But there is a plot at work,
mastered by spiders
and strange, unseen birds.

Not a fable.........certainly not,
but if you are momentarily distracted
by a pluck upon your web,
you will miss the meaning.

You are not the protagonist.

The world is full of villains

and precious is the insult
of your unlikely dénouement.

Breaking the World Record in the Silent Treatment

Erin Bealmear

Your favorite piece of punctuation
was always the ellipsis, a convenient method
of omitting the unsaid, it once impregnated
the pages of your letters. Now, after years
of silence, I often wonder if you've become one,
a typographical symbol for a mirage. In my mind,
I envision some bizarre literary hybrid,
a cross between the *Chicago Manual of Style*
and a Kafka novel, in which you transform
into your own reticence. I imagine that I will
discover you, one day, alone in your dark room,
nothing more than a dot, dot, dot, floating
against the wall.

Labwork

Ire'ne Lara Silva

i gave them
my arm i've found it hurts less
if i watch everything but the exact moment the needle
pierces my vein my blood is a deep almost black red
i watch it being drawn
out of me enough to fill three vials

i remember when my blood was bright
red the red of poinsettias the red
of other people's blood

it's not my imagination, i said to the young nurse, my
blood is darker than it was, isn't it yes, she said, flicking
her ponytail,
it's the insulin

of all the changes diabetes has brought to my body the
sensitivity to heat the painfully dry skin the weight gain
the exhaustion
this change in the color of my blood makes me sad
seems to say i am changed

changed irredeemably
changed without return

what else of me has changed
what would i tell the lover now the one who said my
skin carried the scent of sunlight and maíz the one who
murmured against my thighs that i tasted of night
jasmine
and the earth after rain

do i taste of illness now of medications
acid and poison is my skin marked over with toxic
warnings no lover now could know my body young or
strong or healthy no lover now could know the taste of
me before insulin before disease

is this still my body to give
and who would find this body beautiful
when i can't even
recognize it

Depression: An Interrupted Sestina

no one said the darkness only subsides
never disappearing   never dying
it is no ocean   it is no river
intermingling with my blood   it is my blood
my inheritance my ancestral memory
my first word   my last   the words   in between

i eat   i sleep   i dream   i rage   between
fogs   i even speak light till it subsides
a hundred songs to sing from memory
forgetting pain   forgetting all dying
i love   i give   i touch   i dance   my laughing blood
flowing in a bright burning river

but the next day   pours lies   pours filth   into the river
of my sleep   and there is a wall between
me and the world   the air tastes of blood
dust and rage   i don't remember what subsides
impossible to grasp   all the things that are dying
insisting insisting   abandon this memory

all lights
speak of stars
all stars
speak of living
but
all stars die

where
is
respite refuge rest
pain without end
hurting
outside myself
sinking
in through my skin

all stars
speak of silence
silence
sings the longest song
but all stars die

what is memory
to
this body
mothered
by
sadness

you don't know dying   you can't touch memory
listen to your whispering blood   find the river
breathe slowly in-between   wait till it subsides

The World is Medicine

let it in
the sunshine the rain the wind the lightning
                         eat the raw
                         eat the stones and eat the marrow
                                   eat the warmth on your skin
                                   and the words the sun is writing
            eat the scent of the earth after rain
            eat the storm the thunder rumbling inside

this is how you grow strong
be the roar be the keening
      be the screaming be the running
      be louder
                         be the wind be the trees growing tall
                         be the word be the day be the knife
be the hot rush of blood
be the clouds
                              be the electric spill of blooming
                              flowers in the desert
begin
and end with water
            never forget

the ocean lives inside us

the rivers take us

where our ancestors walked

our bodies still ebb and flow

with the tides

there is no joy like the joy of the body

suspended in water weightless and fierce

water is life

drink it in .

touch the world eat the world be the world

the world is medicine

I Prefer to Be

John McKernan

The gleam
In my father's eye

Or several wayward
Blood cells coasting
Towards my mother's breasts

Tomorrow's my fiftieth birthday
I plan to spend many hours
Walking miles along Davis Creek
Staring at chicory & goldenrod

I'm exhausted
Impersonating myself
Of being two years old forever
Of trying to peel my photo
Off all those milk cartons

What Will Suffice

Anthony Fife

Sandwiched between the night
and morning, spying the heatless
first light fill my wide sky
bottom up, like water in a cup.

Such bird song—such chatter
on top of chatter, each voice lost
within the fabric of each voice loud,
heading home from the early shift.

It is enough to be here, but play
no part. It is enough to
observe, and be stone nameless
beneath the white glare of unblinking sky.

With the Wind

After William Stafford

The unwanted—they have such
avenues. So many roads
to go. No one knows the difference,

will lift a hand to help or slap them back.
Lorene—she chose to go,
never told a soul about her dream of leaving.

Why not?—she flew this coop and disappeared.
The unwanted?—sometimes you just are.
Then someone calls your name—you answer.

Maybe this is wishful thinking (the laces
of her flying shoes sewn tight), but
I bet she never looked back,
I bet she never stopped.

How to Fold a Map

K. A. Wisniewski

Who still needs a map?
Driving *up* to see you
doesn't mean I'm moving north
anymore. Nobody reads
legends, and the compass
may appear in analog on some screen
but nobody pays it much mind.

We all know the shape of the earth.
Round, like a ball. One-sided.
The old road maps paint a better picture.
Various sides tucked away
inside each other.
Flat, creased, balled-up.
Nobody really rolls
unless they're on holiday, perhaps
preparing to scream at some theme park.

We could complain or brag
on where we've been,
dream or dread where we're going,
argue about the meaning of signs.

But we're all on the same side,
aren't we?

I'll worry that I've forgotten the map.
You'll be disappointed
when I want to read it.
We'll follow the shoreline
until there are no more roads,
and I wish I'd brought the map.
But two people with a map
can still be lost: losing lines
in creases and finding new ones.

Home is a special place.
The same as when we left it.
Even with our different route back.
I'd lecture about how to fold a map.
It might be the same size as before,
but it's lines will never quite line up the same.
New points lay on new points.

Sirenum Scopuli in Terra Australis

Shane Kash

The LC-130 banks sharply to the right. I am on the starboard side of the aircraft and feel like I am lying on my back. A slight nausea washes over me as I have no visual reference. The Air Force crew member holds up three fingers to indicate that we will be landing in three minutes. The fuselage has no windows and no sound dampening qualities. There would be no way to talk to the person next to me if there were anyone else there besides the single National Science Foundation director sent out to make sure everything is in order. After a short time the plane shudders as the skis touch down unseen on the ice runway and begins to slow. The cargo door in the rear opens like the gaping maw of some metal whale. Still in motion, a light up by the crew member changes from red to green and the several tons of cargo, stacked to the ceiling and occupying the rest of the space inside the craft, unexpectedly lurch forward on their slave-pallets and slide out onto the ice. The plane continues as the doors slowly close, and we taxi up to where I get out. Exiting through the aircraft door, I am presented with the absolute height of my life's travels: the Central Transantarctic Mountain Camp, CTAM for short.

Stepping out onto the ice of the glacier that the camp is situated on, I am ushered off of the airstrip past the huge fuel bladders. The fuelies are already at work dragging lines out to the airplane to prepare it for its flight back. The cargo staff is retrieving the slave pallets from the runway and reloading the craft. Waiting for me is one of my coworkers with whom I am rotating positions with. She shows me the basic layout of the camp and the Quonset style tent that serves as the galley that I will be working in. While being introduced to the three chefs ,whom I will be working for, I am shown what other facilities are located in the camp, including the medical tent, air-ops tent for coordinating the helicopters and bush planes, and the most interesting outhouses I will ever use. Simply put, they are the classic looking outhouses complete with crescent moon on the door but situated over an 80 foot shaft melted directly straight down into the glacier. Finally, I am presented with my housing accommodation: a small red tent, barely large enough to lay diagonal in, dug in and dead-manned[1] into the ice amongst the few dozen other tents in the tent city. It's even smaller than the cramped conditions at McMurdo Station[2] that I left this morning. Though tiny, it is perfect.

A few minutes later the sound of the LC-130's propellers increase and I watch it lumber down the airstrip. Its mass lifts gently up into the east horizon and leaves me enveloped in the still, loud silence of Antarctica. No sound, no scent, just an amazing cloudless blue sky and intense sunlight reflected off of an unbroken sheet of white in almost all directions.

Situated on the Bowden Neve at an altitude of about 6000 feet, CTAM is "located just north of the mighty Beardmore Glacier, nearly 400 miles from McMurdo" (Rejcek), 84°south latitude, about

---

1 Dead-manning is the practice of burying the ends of the tent guy lines instead of the classic method of staking them. It ensures greater stability in high wind, a frequent occurrence in Antarctica.

2 McMurdo Station is the largest of the Antarctic research stations and a jump off point for almost all field camps for the United States.

400 miles from the South Pole Station. With a scattering of tents and equipment-laden pallets, the site is tucked into a cirque of the mountain ridge to our south with the vast expanse of the glacier itself extending to the east toward the distant Queen Alexandra Range (Owen 312). It is a camp that is set up about every six to ten years by the National Science Foundation for a multitude of research studies, including geomagnetic analysis and NASA's search for meteorites. The primary purpose, however, is for paleontology. These scientists have been progressively recovering several animals, some 250 million years old, from the surrounding hills for the past 25 years. This is where I will spend the next two weeks as a kitchen assistant. I will spend Christmas 2010 and New Years here this year. I will play kickball on Christmas Eve with some of the foremost scientists in their fields, all while the camps director walks the bases with a bottle of Maker's Mark filling empty cups. I will learn to tell the time in the middle of the night by the position of the sun, which never sets, on my tent wall. Slowly, steadily the cavitations of helicopter blades break the silence as one of the choppers comes back to camp with an inbound team. I am exactly where I want to be.

Back in May that year, while perusing the ads for food service jobs on Craigslist, I came across one that simply read "food service in Antarctica." This location was one that I have always had a deep fascination with, the intrigue was too great, and with my wife's encouragement, I simply had to apply. To my great joy and surprise and two interviews later, I found myself hired for a 5-month deployment for the 2010-11 science season at McMurdo Station in Antarctica and prepared to leave in September. After a long series of medical tests and vaccinations to ensure that I was physically qualified, the day arrived, and off I went.

I was first flown to Denver, the United States Antarctic Program's base of operations, for orientation, and then very quickly back onto a plane bound for Christchurch, New Zealand. In New Zealand, we were outfitted with extreme cold weather gear. As soon as conditions on the ice in Antarctica permitted, I was put back onto a plane for a five hour flight to Pegasus Airfield at McMurdo Station. I was 12,000 miles from my home base, and I was finally able to plant my feet onto the continent of Antarctica and cross it off my lifetime travel list.

At the station, my job was dining attendant. In short, we took care of the galley and dining facility. The chefs made food for the 1,200 personnel; the dining attendants made sure it was available and that everything stayed clean. The work was somewhat repetitive, but the camaraderie made up for it. In talking to one of my managers one afternoon, I learned of this specific field camp and that it was possible to be deployed there from the McMurdo Station. He told me about the dinosaur fossils that scientists were uncovering. I decided then and there that I was going—I had to go! I also learned that there were only three spots available for the position; the selection would be merit based. Well, either I performed better or they all performed worse, but on December 15th, the day after my birthday, I was informed that in two days I would be sent out into the field—truly a dream come true, a chance to go further.

There exists in those of us, for whom travel is as essential as food, water, or air, a fire that needs to be fed. It is a need to see more, to go further, and to experience the authentic. It is one thing to go to a remote Pacific island and stay in a luxury suite, and that's all fine, but it is quite another to see how people live there. Some of us regard tourism as, well, for tourists, and for ourselves, contradictorily, as something else. When the opportunity presents itself, we that thirst for this experience can hear its siren song and must pursue its call by any means necessary.

Arriving at this field camp, there is no doubt this it is as far from tourism as possible. It is something out of a movie, although for real. I am in a place that so few people know exists, much less will ever go to, that I could fit them all in a movie theater. At this moment, I can rest in the self-satisfaction of having achieved the most exotic locale I may ever experience.

When I started all of this, I could not have possibly dreamed I would have ended up here. McMurdo Station alone, the original goal, would have been enough, but here I am. By simply seizing an opportunity that I knew would never be available again, I ended up much further than I expected. It is much better to live and learn than not and regret it. Despite my detractors, their criticism, and the lists of "reasons not to go," I've forged ahead. My confidence is sky high. My fire is lit. Standing here next to my little tent, glacier glasses on, staring at the Fata Morgana[3] on the horizon, I can feel it in my gut. It has all been worth it.

---

3 Fata Morgana are mirages that occur as a the result of light and temperature refraction. They are somewhat common in Antarctica and can make mountains appear upside down, larger than they actually are, stretched, and in locations they are not.

Works Cited

Owen, R.E. "Second Special Antarctic Issue." *New Zealand Journal of Geology and Geophysics* 6.3 (1963): 312. Print.

Rejcek, Peter. "Mountain Life: CTAM camp staff works behind the scenes to support science." *The Antarctic Sun.* USAP. 15 April 2011. Web. 16 Jan. 2013.

City Rhino

James Grabill

In the gray light, mid-morning, the rhino's still standing, taking in the
rock and gray air.

As she yawns, the great grain elevator in back of her tongue drips, the
air whistling in Kenyan with dragonflies over head-high grasses.

At the corner of the eye, ancient kinship branches. Gray calendars
count with presence not numbers, or the Pacific rhino home
stands naked, stopped in rolling alien scan.

Molecular light passes into blood-making marrow, but what's new?
The close-by parallel world edges up, but who remembers?

Not much to be done. Water, food, inside, out still arrive.

Boots sagging, concrete crumbling out of sight for decades, the rhino
tips her horn in the vacant garage, the year the mechanic took
off.

Where branches are kept impossible to see.

Afternoon sky cuts quick as it merges with the long story. The path returns but never left. The split of a seismic fault might start where the salt-sea boils.

In a Brushstroke of Hair

The search for lit blossoms at the end of possessions could reveal what
Picasso painted in a city of weight-bearing mirrors.

The immense flag of craters of the moon can have the reach of pre-
emptive Buber when *us* encompasses *them*.

The beautiful ideological marble gymnasiums with golden balls and
fierce bone-white tattooing of the small of ankles could be the
chance to admit a billion slender latitudes of stars.

Any unnamed mayflies hatching in scientific Brazil on its ripening root
will stay ignited from genetically encrypted nerve.

Wants of the moment that have landed after fashionable TB, pounds
of whip-snapping roll and rake where a wave turns, grim services dealing Tarot cards out into lives on the line may all have
satellites grazing.

So the rain weight in a bursting sunflower seed finds its balance.

And the indivisible further edge of descendants under the sky will have
    Eleanor Roosevelt on a WWII carrier reassuring the young, un-
    til you can hear the snap and boom of canvas sails on the old
    sea.

The Engineer's Fiber

All we need is a bridge connecting the level ground here to level ground there.

The design should speak the language of both natural and public architecture. Arcing, suspended within time, the bridge must be self-supporting, its plumb cables interwoven with diagonal arrays of lines descending mathematically through the atmosphere.

Late-afternoon light passing through the cables would be sound, prisming in strings of this immense symphonic instrument. To the canyon, the bridge would be a feather, light and mostly unseen, its strength designed to outlast utility.

Its carbon fiber, the result of experiments of cells, will be stronger than steel, grown out of long-term technology of the genome, giving it beauty in sync with its circumstances.

All we need is a symbolic creation capable of bearing our weight over the long-term gap dividing the world into disciplines.

There Is Nothing Left

Holly Day

I don't want to answer the door anymore except for the mail,
and when I do, I smile, I smile at the mailman for my mail, I smile at
     my husband
I smile at everyone at everyone. my face hurts from smiling so much.

my hands over my stomach, protecting nothing. I shuffle through
my days, or is it one long, endless day, find comfort
in repetitive tasks. I vacuum constantly.
I find myself talking to the missing baby, crochet tiny mittens
meant for baby hands, pass them on to friends with children

turn inside myself

hold back everything but this smile, the one I show my family
everyone. I thank everyone for their kindness and for the flowers.
I want to let the tiny wreaths pile up, wither away.
my husband compliments me on my strength, I
have nothing left to say.

At *Dejima* Wharf

Jonathan Greenhause

Water from Nagasaki Bay laps gently against the docks,
              where restaurants are lined up,
    each one
boasting separate musical acts   & culinary specialties
like the noodle shop offering a Hawaiian-style rock n' roll band
              as its owner offers a spirited *Let's go!*
      before the lead guitarist introduces his cascading notes
              into the salt-tinged air,
      & a woman sings
    Enka's country-music twang
              from a sushi joint
        as her toddler claps his hands   joyously out of rhythm.

Moored ships silently await the dawn to lift anchor,
              their barnacled hulls
    disappearing & reappearing
            with the kiss of each new wave,
      while past the boardwalk
a park in shadow shelters a night bird as it calls   so hushed & sweet
      it throws reclusive lovers   into reveries beneath the trees,
              & adolescents
        illuminate the air with lighters & handheld sparklers

beneath fireworks blasting in branched explosions of gold, red, &
        green,
                        as light dispels darkness
        & old men watch the blinking lights of boats no longer there.

The Nagasaki Bridge is draped in artificial stars suspended
                        like a periwinkle dress,
        & a foghorn bellows its baritone as wooden planks creak.
Lapping waves somehow seem eternal,   as couples stroll hand-in-
        hand,
                                their imprints & shadows
                etched forever
in the boardwalk's tactile memory
                        in this dark night
                inebriated   by a cloak of redemption & desire.

A Speck

Lowell Jaeger

We're craning our necks, heads
pressed against the window glass, tracking
a glinting speck of sunlit wings,
till it shrinks and blinks out
in the haze-blue sky.

He'd kissed
Mom and each of us
goodbye. He'd waited beside us
on the plastic seats, bought us
each a Coke, kept checking his watch.

And before that, he'd dropped
eight quarters in a machine on a far wall
of the terminal—flight insurance—
one thousand dollar accidental death
payout. A bundle of cash back then,
enough to cover funeral expenses,
he said, and a car payment or two.

Mom wouldn't touch it.
So he slipped the papers in her purse

and clicked it shut.
As loudspeakers called passengers to board.
As the plane's great props stuttered,
then caught, then roared.

Ode to Laziness

John Walser

Pablo, la pereza visited me
yesterday morning
like a bareground shadow
under an ornamental shrub

and left me precious nothing:

no twig, no basil seeds,
no lake polished stones,
no legs entwined in mine
as we spun along the coastline
of some dance floor.

I had only the cicada song
of a neighbor's air conditioner

and I lay on the living room floor
my pillow thick with inactivity's sweat.

The cracking voices of small birds—
sparrows, swallows, larks,

ones I cannot name—
turmoiled in the heavy trees.

The sky, the old grey of melted wax:

sometimes I moved to the other room;
sometimes I did not.

I wish, like you, Pablo,
on the cover of your book
I just pulled from a shelf

I could press my hands together
in prayer or celebration,
the victor in black and white,
who, at the beginning of another day,
ivy-capped and content, greets himself
the way I cannot right now.

And that figurehead
that hovers over your shoulder,
over your workshop,
that sings back the song of waves on the rocks,
her breasts and shoulders almost bare,
she promises you what, Pablo?
topaz? phoebe eggs? black tea?

At Christmas time when I was a small child
the oranges came in a cardboard crate

shipped from where you stand,
the grapefruit individually wrapped in paper,
separated by plastic rebirth grass:
a surprise, a gift.

Is this what I—amigo de las tormentas—
am waiting for now:
a purchase of the sun?

Pablo, I did not notice it seep,
the heated metal of the day,
through my open windows,
not as blare and drip as July,
when every movement of sky,
tree limbs, crows' wings
is liquid and long

but still the lethargy of heat,
the arithmetic of heat,
the complex division of heat on my body.

When I melt away, I am portioned
not by a constant
but by an ever shifting variable

like the number of tiny spiders
that hatch from the webs strung
along my balcony eaves.

How they parachute against the wind.

See now how the sky curdles before sunset.
See the seabird feather clouds.
See how a hummingbird pirates dew.

What I am trying to say, Pablo,
is I don't know why I'm telling these things,
this place, this moment.
What I am trying to say
is this is not about a shift of wind,
the ocean currents,
not about the angle of the sun.
It is my husk and meat, my pulp and cell.

At eight already tonight the cage of the sky
has been blanket covered
to stop the daybirds from scratching out
stylus sounds with their crisp and dry beaks.

And I fear that tomorrow again
and the next day and the next
I will be here, clay grey,
talking to you

not shuffling mussel shells in my palm,
not wading into the low-tide minnow shallows,

not studying the peppers and berries
at the farmers market,
the oranges and olives,
the red-gilled fish laid out on piles of ice,

not drawing my finger, pollen stained,
along the purple lashes of a passion flower,
not following the shingle shift of her hips.

Survival

T Jay McCollum

Waning light with waxing days,
Brings more darkness into every place.
And as the cold bites the flesh,
Sanity slips through your mental mesh.

Now in the chasm of some age-old crater,
If you want to live, it's now not later.
This mountain is your final test,
Living will prove that you're best.

Light is scarce, that days are long,
But you haven't given up, you'll keep moving on.
Even through this torrent of wind and storm,
Tired and hungry, your spirit torn.

And in the end, you'll never guess,
You feel your body less and less.
The numbing feeling constricts your mind,
Eternal sleep in this icy bind.

One Last Meal

Carl W. Graham

My mother was an excellent cook. While she had more than a few cookbooks around the house, the only one she really used was her big *Betty Crocker Cookbook* that seemed to be her primary guide for doing anything from roasting a turkey to baking bread. For everything else, she had her notebooks. These half dozen or so wonderfully disorganized dream books were a colorful assortment of 8 by 10 spiral notepads filled with all manner of recipes gathered from friends, family, and *Parade Magazine*, all written down in her precise handwriting. In one, you might encounter a recipe for sweet and sour pineapple chicken cooked over rice right next to a recipe for zucchini bread our Finnish neighbor Elsie Osmanberg shared with her as the two of them drank coffee together one winter afternoon in 1972. While my mom never kept a formal diary, these books served that function in their own way, filled with all the food that she cooked or wanted to cook, a rough guide to who she was and wanted to be in the kitchen. A guide I can't bear to look at now because it breaks my heart.

It's hard for me to believe that she's been gone for 20 years. I can clearly see Mom whenever I smell the yeasty scent of freshly baking bread, elbows deep in a doughy mass, turning and kneading, pounding her magic on her flour-covered kitchen counter. She is so vibrant, full of life and energy and promise. One bakes bread because there is a future where bread can be eaten and shared with people you love.

Bread is hope, it is life and it is the promise of warmth and comfort. No other idea of bread occurred to me until two years ago when my aunt, my mother's sister, shared a terrible secret with me.

Like many things in life I can't pinpoint the moment the change happened. One day my mother was someone who baked bread and the next she wasn't. Months may have passed before the inevitable happened and I developed a very strong craving for her cinnamon rolls, huge fat glistening rolls packed with insane amounts of molten brown sugar and raisins, and I casually asked my mom if she would make me some.

"Oh, you'd like that wouldn't you," my mother said "do you want me to be fat? Is that what you want?"

The sudden anger in her voice shocked me. So did the word *fat*. The fact of the matter was she was fat, and so was I: we were two fat people in a family of skinny people. My mother's obesity was just an accepted certainty in my universe; she had always been that way for as long as I could remember. I had only seen a handful of black-and-white photographs to prove she had ever been anything else, a slightly embarrassed smiling young woman on the day of her high school graduation and some pictures taken soon after she had married my dad: glamorous, handsome pictures of a well-dressed thin woman who looked directly into the camera. Pictures that neither my brother nor I felt comfortable looking at because they were not pictures of the woman who raised us, the one we remember, the one we loved, the fat one—only you didn't call her that if you wanted to live for very long afterward.

The word fat when applied toward my mother was forbidden in our household by unspoken agreement. I do not know what would have happened if any of us had spoken it out loud within her hearing, but I deeply suspect, suspect down to my bones, that something, whatever it was, would not be good. Not good in the sense that a tornado in a trailer park is not good. Not good in a way that none of us in that household, including my dad, was willing to find out. The fact that she spoke the F-Word out loud was more deeply shocking to me than I can relate, so shocking all I could do at the time was mumble an apology and swear to myself that I would never bring up her baking anything ever again for as long as I lived.

And I was true to my word. I never did ask her to bake anything again. I thought about it, remembering her homemade dinner rolls and warm thick-sliced bread and luscious fruit pies as only a fat boy can, but I never gathered up the courage to ask her to make any of them ever again. Oh on occasion, like on a birthday she might bake a Duncan Hines cake or roll out a pie shell on Thanksgiving, but for the most part her days of large-scale take over the kitchen baking were over.

Or so I thought until my Aunt Faith told me my mother's secret.

My aunt, always the brave one in our family, asked my mother one day over the phone why she was still heavy when she never really saw her eating anything all that fattening at home. My mother replied, my aunt told me, that when my dad was at work and the boys were in school she would bake herself some bread or cinnamon rolls and eat it all herself and clean up the all the evidence before any of us got home. The image of her, standing alone in her kitchen, performing a sort of Reverse Sacrament, transforming the bread from a symbol of life and health into one of shame and humiliation, is too painful to contemplate.

As every fat person knows, the act of eating is not simply to support life. We eat for many reasons, many of them emotional, as we go about our daily lives. We eat because we are happy, we eat because we are sad, and we eat because we are bored. Often, we eat when we are not even hungry or even because the food is all that appealing: it's just something we do. And sometimes, like my mother, we eat in secret. I call this *shame eating* because many are the times that I have stopped and bought a box of donuts or a large bag of burgers and eaten them all before I even got home, throwing away the bag or the box before I reached my front door in as casual and unthinking an act of self-sabotage as I can think of, and one that would kill me with humiliation if any of my friends or family were to witness it. The thought of my mother, doing essentially the same thing, and probably feeling the same self-loathing and guilt as I did on these occasions, fills me with pity. A sentiment, I'm sure, she would have hated.

That we shared so much in common, my mother and I, would not become apparent to me until many years after her death. Our relationship with food, as with each other, was, in a word, complicated. So complicated, in fact, I'm still unraveling it now.

My mother received a crushing blow in 1983 with the death of my father, a loss she never fully recovered from. It is as if we buried part of her alongside my dad on the day of his funeral because the woman who sought out recipes and food ideas for her notebooks never seemed to resurface. While not all the negative changes were immediate, they gradually began to take hold of her and no amount of energy on my part could change it. You see, I had moved back home to be with her during my father's terminal session with cancer and I didn't leave again until we sold the house after my mother's. I was there for the whole 10-year cruise, and despite my best efforts I have some doubts now about whether I actually helped in steering that doomed ship my mother and I found ourselves on.

Let me sum it up this way: my mother became depressed, so depressed she didn't leave the house for the last seven years of the ten she had left in her life. In the meantime, I did my best to pretend that everything was all right, did my best to care for her, even after her stroke, and above all else, I did my best to distract my mother from her pain. Chief amongst those distractions was, you guessed it, food. If food could act as a balm to heal her pain, I applied it to my mother's wounds with a shovel.

About once a week I would take her out to dinner, and when she could no longer bear to leave the house, I brought those dinners home to her. I made it my personal mission to seek out new tastes such as exotic Asian cuisine and seafood delicacies and bring them home to her because the food we were eating there was becoming more and more bland, such as boiled pasta with straight from the jar sauce and pot after pot of brown rice, as her interest waned in preparing any of the recipes from her notebooks. As I look back on it, I think these meals and some of the colorful foods I tried to cook in her kitchen were as much for me as for her, giving me the illusion that I could change our situation if I could just find the right dish or discover the correct seasoning that would make her happy again. I realize now how foolish that sounds; even as I write these words on paper, I am profoundly disturbed by them. Desperate people sometimes believe foolish things.

Finally, the last illness arrived, and just as she had been predicting for years, it was cancer. That was about where her premonitions ended however because her reaction to her situation was almost the polar opposite of what she had told me it would be over many an awkward and uncomfortable conversation. Instead of giving in to the disease and opting out of any futile treatments and painful procedures she fought the disease with everything she had. She took every medical option the doctors offered her, both chemo and radiation, grasping at any straw that presented itself no matter how tenuous it was. After all those years of longing for an end she discovered she wanted to live after all.

Mom had been in a coma for several days when one morning she simply woke up, woke up as if from a nap and not a downward spiral into death. I came into her room that morning to find her awake and telling me she was hungry. I hadn't heard her say the word *hungry* in a long time because appetite is often the first casualty of cancer. When I asked her what she wanted she told me shrimp without hesitation, so shrimp, after a doctor said it couldn't hurt, I bought. The doctor said one last thing before I headed out to a Chinese restaurant, that it was a miracle she was awake, but it wouldn't last. He told me if I had any final arrangements to make with her to do them now because she would eventually lapse back into her coma and I would never get this opportunity again. All this he told me as if he was just a little disappointed in her that she wasn't dying on schedule.

I bought the shrimp, laid it out on the funny half table that straddles the hospital bed and had dinner with my mom one final time. Please don't ask me how it tasted or how wonderfully it was prepared. For once in my life I didn't care. All I remember clearly was what we talked about. We talked about when she would get better and what we would do when we got back home. A few hours after we ate she got tired, went to sleep and died the next day.

Three Guys

Jeffrey Zable

Three guys are sitting on a bench
evaluating women on their physical
characteristics as they walk by.

Half the time the evaluations are made
with facial expressions that range from
stinky faces, to raised lower lips
which obviously means that the woman
shows promise.

All of these guys are from another country,
and though I know which one, it's not
really important. They could be from
anywhere men are found.

As I continue to watch them I get the feeling
that all three of these guys have trouble
with women, and if any of them gets laid,
it's probably by the same women
who made them express their displeasure
with stinky faces.

Your Time Will Come

Brian C. Felder

Mild as it may be
in comparison to other, snowier years,
it is still winter in this place we call home,
so we revert to our cold weather routines.
We lie abed long into the morning, coffee in hand,
reading our books and magazines,
any thoughts about the day ahead deferred indefinitely.
We are retired and no longer respond to a master's call,
the promise of a reward holding no sway over us.
In time, we will rise and shower and dress
and go about our business,
for there are always chores to be done
and groceries to be laid in
and mail to be picked up and dealt with or not,
but, soon, it will be late afternoon
and we will light our fire and build a drink
and sit down to play yet another game of Scrabble
or ink the crosswords we have saved for such a moment.
We do not want our minds to become dull
in the absence of greater demands upon them,
but my wife and I do not miss work.

Neither will you when your hour comes,
especially when winter closes in
and both the days and years grow short.

Vancouver Woman Beats Her Husband To Death With A Hammer

William Jolliff

The Oregonian, May 31, 2012

So how many times do you have to say,
"Don't leave those greasy dirty tools
on the dining room table, Sweetheart"?
Well, I guess somebody knows now.
At least he knew for half a minute.

Maybe he made the related mistake
of leaving his greasy tool on the bed.
Maybe he had it coming. Or maybe
he had it coming on some other bed.

It's a sad comment on these weird
and decadent days we die in.
What's become of the old-lace grace,
the gentility, of arsenic with tea?
Granted, critics call it sentimental.

You could take a more direct approach.
There's something akin to tenderness

in a .38 placed against a graying temple,
dreaming sweetly of sugar plums.

Either way, the corpse could be a problem.
But since he always loved the garden so,
well, maybe he can stay there—it's poetry.
Think about him when you pull a turnip.
Whisper a little prayer. Say grace.

Or this: How about a broken brake-line?
You can use his own damn coping saw
if, with that mess he leaves in the garage,
you can find it. Vancouver has plenty of hills.

Toss in some drama, a little pizzazz:
Call up the cop shop around midnight.
I'm so worried, he didn't come home,
he's never, never late...Please, please....
If theatre was never quite your shtick,

just hire a pro. There's simplicity
as well as commercial expediency
in a hired gun with a Heckler & Koch.
It's pricey, but you're buying a memory.

If that doesn't trip your trigger, maybe
you're destined to stick with tradition:

pure, icy contempt, dripping slowly,
silently, consistently for a long, long time.
But there's a certain mercy in a hammer.

Oblique

Jeanine Stevens

So pleased to be out early,
the young mother wears
her new white gloves.
In the brisk winter sun,
she pins fresh laundry,
prefers the make-shift clothesline
and the wood pegs that gently
hold her little boy's shirts,
not like the spring-pins
that crimp delicate fabrics.
She wonders if the grazing deer
she saw yesterday notice
the smoky fragrance of autumn leaves.
Her hands reach up with the last
bed sheet, bright and quick.
With his expensive scope,
the hunter is certain
he sees the white scut, spots
the white flag for a clean shot.
No one is charged.
The husband in grief
takes his sons away

from the changeable forest
to a prairie where light and shadow
are what they seem
where folks are accountable,
and no one mistakes
a buffalo for a locomotive.

A Paris Reading at the End of the Occupation

After Simone de Beauvoir

I'm invited to a reading of Picasso's play, *Desire Caught
by the Tail*, hosted by an Argentine millionaire.

(We had to amuse ourselves somehow, even crosswords
were banned, they might pass on secret codes.)

All the parts were taken, Big Foot, Thin Misery, The Tart,
applauded by Sartre and Camus with great enthusiasm.

Picasso brought an elegant chocolate gateau.
Someone pointed out a gorgeous man...Georges Braque.

I fussed over what to wear, to Picasso's delight,
borrowed a red angora sweater and big blue pearls.

Our hosts kept us past curfew, we stayed the night.
It was pre-mature gaiety. The city had become

a vast gloomy Stalag, but a sense of freedom hung
about avenues, monuments and prisoner's barracks.

We heard the allies were in Italy, Rome was
next. All over Paris, drawings of a snail

crawled up the Italian coastline
in English and American national colors.

There was enough wine left for more scenes.
In darkness, we tasted victory, a stealthy pleasure.

And mornings, a good time to be out, once again
greeted by the warmth of fresh yeasty bread.

Decide

Leesha R. White

Decide,
who is wrong,
what is right.

Decide,
will you flee
or will you fight.

Trust your heart,
trust the night
for wings can only be unfurled
while falling from great heights.

Reflected

Youthful minds walk
dream paths of gold
where perfume drenches the air.
Along the way...
age surmises the journey
reflects the mirroring lake
floats the solitary canoe,
spun then turned
shattered by wind

The Old Man at the Bike Shop

John P. Kristofco

he worked in back with wrenches, rags,
not showroom's sea of shining wheels,
whirling spandex fantasies,
thirty gears waiting for the lean and draft,
bank into the angle of the yellow,
red, the pack,
ten thousand dollar daydream
demons down the mountain,

not there

but back with greasy fingered
rim and wire,
polishing with hands that once held
Huffy's three-speed changers
rusted with the rain of baseball, backyards,
best bike he had ever seen, still,
there because the riding wind
had never left his face,
three score year and ten endangered eagle,

flying, still,
protected in the refuge
of this sacred place

Grandmother

Pennsylvania

In your final summer I was nine
and coming

      down

          the

              steps

        for

      breakfast

at the table by the sink,

lacelike little woman, Mary,
apron tied against your flowered dress,
bony hands folded at the waist,
holding in the days and nights
of coal mines and eleven kids,
shadings of a soul I'd never know,

standing at the window
to your modest mountain's
morning sun

falling on the two of us alike,
warming us together
with the wisdom
of its ancient light

Ghost in the Elevator

Jessica Lilien

It was hard to know how long he'd been there, before we noticed him. He was just one more body in the elevator, one more face to smile vaguely toward without seeing, one more personal bubble to avoid popping at 8:58am and 5:11pm (or 6:32pm or 12:01am—depending on who you were, who you worked for, who you knew would still be there to see when you left for the day, who you needed to impress). Even after we noticed, it wasn't something that was particularly easy to bring up or ask each other about. It wasn't that we were *embarrassed*, exactly (though maybe some of us were), but it was just so hard to actually put into words, even to ourselves. It was hard enough to realize that there was a question to be asked, much less to think of what it should be, or to whom we might eventually put it. So it's hard to tell just how long he'd been here at the Firm. We thought we remembered him from back when we first started, but maybe we only remembered stories we'd heard, or told.

The story, or question, probably first planted itself in the moist, dark soil of the Administrative Group (they usually do), where it itched down to root in their intricate system of long lunches and clandestine instant messages and off-network e-mails. Who knows how long it had there to flower into something that already, even then, had its branching, divergent histories? Maybe the first time the AG let the rest of us in on it was the summer that the young ambitious night-school

MBA's in HR decided to throw the "Friday Floor Fetes" for "community-building" and "moral-expansion" the "raising of employee-Firm fealty." It was the first time, as far any of us, even those of us who had been there the longest, could remember, that the different pay grades and castes really got to talking, chatting casually, comparing notes, talking about him.

Keeley MacLeod had a little paper plate in one hand, grapes and wheat crackers. She wasn't drinking the free cheap(ish) wine. She was pregnant, but only just barely, and she hadn't told any of us yet; we hadn't planned a party for her yet.

"He's not dressed so professional—like the associates in *my* department," she was saying, shooting meaningful, flirty eye contact to Katherine Birbraun from underneath her eyelashes (Katherine, *old*, way overdue for retirement, one of the first full female partners in the state, fucking *hardcore*, rolled her eyes and waved her hand and *blushed*), "but the fact remains that he's in a *suit*. Just, you know, not a very good one." She punched one of the summer kids—from Contracts, not even our floor, just scamming the party for free booze—and asked him, "Maybe he's a Summer Associate, Alec?" (Keeley did that, knew people, knew people's names, god, we missed her when she didn't come back after maternity leave; it happens, even these days, even in a progressive firm like ours.)

It was something we'd all known for—ever. It just took someone else mentioning it first to make us aware. He really *had* always been there, hadn't he? We just hadn't noticed him until—all of the rest of us did, too.

And that night, leaving the office, he was there again. We were extra-careful not to look at him this time; he was more present and less visible than ever. He was an old man in the corner already on the elevator when we entered, no matter what floor we got in on, riding the whole way with us, and never getting off, and never speaking. He was wearing a blue suit, Kevin Etter said, but everybody from Editing swore it was middle-brown, tweed. (And, you know: Editing. We trusted those guys with this kind of thing. They were the English majors, the theatre kids, gay friends with night gigs; it's a stereotype, and we are a progressive firm, but still. They would know, better than Etter, anyway, who was a nice guy, but Tech.) He was old ("Not *old*," Effie Hanover-Price would half-jokingly insist, rolling her eyes and making a goofy face, implying that she herself was old if we thought *he* was, but even she agreed that he was, if not "*old*," at least "old."), grey, white, quiet. He stood in the far back left-hand corner, when we were facing forward. He was hard to see sometimes. He wasn't there, if you looked at him.

"Does he *work* here?" Ritchie asked. Ritchie Castillo was HR, and pretty high up. If he didn't know, then who would?

"He *works* here," Audrey told him, pursed her lips, squinted disapprovingly, walked away without backing it up.

"He doesn't get a paycheck," Ritchie whispered. Only later did any of us think to wonder how Ritchie would have even known his name to be able to look that up.

We thought Kay had spoken to him, because she implied that she had, but nothing came of it.

Once we all knew about him, we thought that Facilities or—Security?—would have to know something. Wasn't that their job? We weren't sure; we weren't, you know, Union. And the Union guys might just not tell us, even if they knew something. There could bad vibes sometimes, between them and us. We didn't do it on purpose, but it happened. It happened everywhere, though—the lawyers didn't talk to us, either.

But none of *us* talked to him, that's for sure. Not that we were *afraid* of him of course; none of us thought he was a—

Maybe he was homeless, riding the elevators all day like a subway car, just blending in somewhere air-conditioned, heated. We asked around. He'd never asked any of us for money, never asked any of us for anything.

We asked around.

Dave Something, he worked the lobby front desk, Security, checked in visitors. He said that this building used to have elevator operators back in the day, handsome black boys (Dave was black, and old, and some of us might have felt a little uncomfortable at this point, but we pretended we weren't, our faces were serious and blank, this is a progressive firm, and *he* was the one who said it, not us) who worked for almost nothing but the uniform and the way their mothers felt when they said their sons had a job, and *here*. He said that back when the elevators went self-serve, sixty-two or -three, one of those elevator operators hung himself, in the shaft, from the top floor, *dangling*. There are still partners here who were there then, they'd confirm it if we asked. They'd know. Just go ask.

We didn't ask.

(Anyway, he wasn't black, and he wasn't young—we were pretty sure; most all of us agreed.)

Or—one woman, one Exec Admin, older, used to be a secretary back when they were *called* secretaries—*she* asked, and she was told that there was a partner, *almost* got his name on the letterhead, but then a case went wrong. Threw himself *down* the elevator shaft. This lawyer who she asked had heard about it from one of the old guys (though he wouldn't say which one).

But that didn't jibe with what everybody in Accounts Payable knew. They all knew a story about a Legal Secretary who'd walked in on you-absolutely-know-who and the SENATOR and who *disap-peared* six days later. (But Accounts Payable talks such a big game about how, hey, maybe he just didn't take the payoff like he should have, is all they're saying, big shrug, not their business, anyway—but these are accounting nerds, not gangsters, nobody believes any of the stuff they say when they're telling stories, pretending to be casual.)

Or just some drone, some nobody in navy blue (or brown tweed), caught in an iffy box between floors, stuck like they get every once in a while, all of us who've been here a while have been on one that jammed, but maybe it just so happens to happen on a Thursday afternoon before a very long holiday weekend, one of those rare ones that comes every now and then, when everybody's so happy to get out to Fire Island or the Hamptons or the homestead and you just starve to death between floors, slowly, sucking the last of your chrome-plated oxygen, cheek-down against the shiny-clean black tile floor, pity the poor custodian who has to find you on Tuesday morning.

He was always there, had always been there. And once we saw him, once everybody was talking about him (Why was it that he was on *every* elevator? There were six elevators. How was it that we could we see him riding more than one at the same time, if we split up and took two different elevators and then compared notes in the lobby?), he was all we could talk about.

And then the talk turned to getting rid of him.

The admins were afraid of him, or said they were. Said he leered at them when they were alone; couple of them said he touched them (though he never touched any of us). And so of course HR said they wouldn't stand anyone, even *him*, making our employees uncomfortable; something had to be done. Security didn't like it, because they didn't know who he was, what he wanted, what he was going to do. It made them look bad. Then the Summer Associates started to *pretend* they couldn't see him, and that was when we knew for sure how the lawyers felt about it. And if *they* wanted him gone that badly, we knew he would be gone soon, somehow.

But you couldn't talk to him. Sweet Maria, Assistant to the Manager of the Administrative Assistants, kind and vaguely religious, or at least really Irish, she said she would try, but then she wouldn't tell us what had happened. If even *she* couldn't convince him to go, then who could? Jessie Wretchell said that Sacco, fourth name on the goddamn letterhead, tried *himself*, *personally*, and got nowhere, and oooh was he mad.

Kay eventually admitted to gay Darren that she only saw him disappear as soon as she got on the elevator, every time.

Custodial deep-cleaned over the long weekend: tried to scrub him out like an odor. But he was there on Tuesday, silent in his corner, gazing expectantly up at the softly binging numbers, waiting forever for his floor.

For a few days, a couple of the Security guys got overtime to ride the elevators all day, just up and down, arms crossed in front of their chests, blandly watching for nothing. Until finally Carla or Horrace or somebody from Accounting told them to knock it off; it wasn't doing any good and it was costing too much money. And it's true: none of those guys saw him, not while they were on the clock.

Word was someone actually wrote up an eviction notice. (Who? Sacco again? Or did they go even higher up this time? Could Meyers have written it himself, like Peter D'Onofrio claimed he did? Is that possible?) A legal document, on good heavy bond, signed and filed and stamped, sealed and ready to be served, but—no one was ever able to serve it.

Someone used the word "exorcism," and we all pretended to laugh, looked away—and made meaningful eye contact with each other the next day when we thought we maybe caught a lingering whiff of sage in the elevator on our ride up. But *he* was there, too. Standing behind us, silently, waiting.

Was he still there when we got off the elevator? Or did he only exist when we were with him? Where would he go, if we ever did manage to get rid of him? Were we really willing to take that responsibility? Of—evicting—him? What had he really done to us, after all, other than make us question him, and his place in the Firm, and the Firm's place in his existence, and the Firm?

It got so we got suspicious: which one of us was *preventing* him from leaving? Which one of us was *keeping* him here, this shameful secret, this evidence of past scandal or malfeasance, this old-fashioned throw-back? *We were a progressive firm.* We couldn't have things like this lingering around in our elevators, cold spots and knockings and chain-rattlings disturbing our clients or—forfend—potential clients.

Kay knew *everyone.* Kay could talk to *anyone.* Why was she claiming now that she'd never even *seen* him? It didn't seem likely, and we started to view her whole schtick—the Russian accent, the flirting, the lunchtime manicures with the boss (hers, ours, whoever's)—with suspicion. It was unseemly. She worked for a partner, it wasn't like she was getting fired or anything, but if we stopped inviting her to the long Friday lunches at the Pig 'N' Whistle or O'Lunney's, that was only because we thought she'd been busy lately, or, you know, sometimes you want to go out with a different group is all.

Or the Summer Associates, always goofing off: you were always catching them asleep under a desk or throwing after-hours parties in a conference room. Nobody expected them to *know* anything, to be able to *help* with him, but who knew what they were actively doing to *keep* him there? With their fratty little pranks and expensive haircuts and cheap suits and their Ivy League gossip message boards. Maybe they thought it was funny. (Had they been the ones who had *brought* him here? No—none of us really believed they had that kind of intellect or power.)

We heard whispers—we don't remember where they first came from, not *our* department—that maybe, if he *was* one of the early partners, maybe that meant he was an old friend of one of the *current* name partners. Because if those guys really *did* want him gone, he'd be gone, right? So maybe we were doing all this work and we were being *deliberately sabotaged* (it wouldn't be the first time—we could name a hundred times—we got that shitty 2% cost-of-living raise just like everybody else last year when we know we deserved more, we know other people got more, we *heard*). We couldn't do anything about it if it was a name partner, even just any partner, it didn't matter, and still they would be blaming us around the clients, deflecting, like they always did.

And the sage thing, anyway—who was that? That had to be Facilities, right? We're not racist or anything, but a lot of them are recent immigrants, from, you know, the Islands or somewhere. Or hell, maybe it was even Angel or Ritchie from HR—those guys were pretty Catholic, and that stuff tended to get weird, too, we knew. Couldn't have been Sweet Maria?

It got to where in order to protect ourselves, we just—left it alone. We didn't want to be blamed for his presence, we didn't want to be dragged down by the theatre fags in Editing or the little girls in Administrative or the idiot Summer kids or the asshole old white men in suits with their names on the stationary (or not)—we didn't want to be associated with any of them, so we just removed ourselves from all of it. He was still there, but we didn't look at him. Or—no, not exactly. Because *that* would have been suspicious. We smiled vaguely at his shape as we entered the elevator every morning at 8:58am and again as we left at 5:11pm (or 6:32pm or 12:01am). We gave him his space and we ignored him, just like we did with the Union guys, just like we did with the woman—Wendy?—who reached past our hip every morning to take our trash can, empty it for us: "Thank you," we said, and she nodded and smiled vaguely at our shape, too, didn't look at us, either—it wasn't just us doing it, it was *all* of us. We all worked here. We were all a part of the Firm. It was by collective agreement. And by the time the Summer Associates left, by the time the Friday Floor Fetes were all over with, by the time fall fell into winter and they were sending out the carefully non-denominational holiday cards, by the time the bonuses has been distributed, whispered about, gossiped over, denied, falsely inflated and posted anonymously to the law school message boards—by that time, he was gone.

Not gone. He wasn't gone. But reintegrated. One of us again. A part of the Firm, invisible, riding the elevators with the rest of us, 8:58am, 5:11pm, lunchtime, coffee break, run to Crumbs to get cupcakes for the baby shower, for the retirement party, run to D'Agostino to get the kind of bottled water the Senator likes. He was there, but so were we, so was Angel, so was Kay, so was Sweet Maria, Dave Something, Katherine Birbraun, Marc Sacco, Kevin Etter, and we didn't know them, either; we didn't ask about them, or at least we didn't listen to their replies. It didn't matter who he was. He was one of us. We were together again, all of us, of one piece again, working together by remaining parts, running smoothly, up and down, floor to floor, back and forth through the very veins of the building, the veins that connected us, fed us, brought us together and apart, moved us through us, made us, kept us alive, kept us working, kept us.

It was a strange rough patch there for a while. But we're all back to work, now, all of us.

Little Pink Houses

Nicole Taylor

Written outside The Little Pink Café in Independence, Oregon

I'm not using a ruler.
I might as well take a photograph. The lady
directly across paints the bright pink frosted house
with Golden acrylics and tells me this.

I hate painting these houses.
I like still-lifes. And she tells me
a few times.

This is what older women do,
learn to paint scenery.

One topped in whitish hair
and in straw hat
painting with thinning watercolors.

They sat near the new cinema
and across from the city's freight office,
Independence Depot.

They paint with Vistas and
Vineyards traveling in the
Willamette Valley on Wednesdays.

My daughter lived here,
one of the managers told me of
this recently moved 1880s house.

Desire in the Pool

Kevin Boyle

As I swim the blue laps between the cords,
I imagine crossing the Hellespont, yelling

"Europe" as I touch the north side, then saying "Asia"
Quietly at the south end, a kind of Marco Polo game

With myself, and all of July I am Leander
As I lap the laps, becoming Hero when I pause,

And I often pause—breath gone, cramps here—
So that as I arrive at shore, sometimes knocking my head

Against the concrete sides, sometimes just stubbing
My fingers, I am the swimmer and the swum to

All in one, lover and beloved, then beloved lover
Until I push off with yearning yet again, spotting

The rotund clock face that is my love's lamp, recalling
After looking it up that the Hellespont is named for

Helle who tumbled into the sea, somehow her fingers
Slipping from the flying ram's fleece as she fled

Her destiny as human sacrifice, which gets me thinking
About not thinking as I swim, just letting it all slip off,

All the dead bodies at the pool's bottom—mythic Greeks,
Real young Turks, barbiturate-laced stars, shot-heavy revelers—

I turn my face from, and as the lovely, toned guards
Blow the whistle each late afternoon to announce thunder,

Lightning far off, coming east by northeast, our way, I wish
To be like Luther and get stung by lightning,

Not sacrificed as in Greek myth, but stung and then
Somehow reshaped, reconfigured, shifting my swim cap some

So it gives me a tonsured look and I monk myself,
Then marry at the last moment a fleeing nun,

The consummation performed dead center between the bride's side
Of gun-whipped Asia, and the groom's side of Europe under siege.

Ash and Clay

When Cinderella met her first cinderblock
She felt a kinship. April had come early
That year, and as she swept and wept,
Wept and swept, she saw the rebar that led
To what the British call a breezeblock
(Because of its many breathing passages)
And the others (Americans, she loved America!)
Called cinderblocks, made from the cinder ash
Of coal and cement. She placed her foot
Inside the block and it fit in a loose way.
If she wore the thick winter socks she had
Just put up in moth balls, perhaps, or
Bent and kept her hands beside her feet,
Perhaps again, but how would she cook and clean,
Sweep and weep? She kissed the blocks
Goodbye, and dreamt of going to Hollywood,

Changing her name back to Aschenputtel—
Cinder Fool or Ash Ass—she liked the ring
Of Ash Ass—and meeting her prince,
But America was a republic without those
Royal trappings, she knew, but still a girl

Could dream! She heard her stepmother
Passing through the breezeway, and got caught
Wondering if the step in stepmother
(A cinderblock, perhaps?) derived from
The Old English *astepan*, to bereave,
And if so, who was the bereaved
If not she Cinderella, Aschenputtel, Ash Ass!

If only her father hadn't died on the ladder
Reaching for the golden apple to give
His new bride after Cinderella's mother, his first wife,
Died on the slope that sloped hard toward
The creek. I am she who is bereft,
Cinderella thought, not this she, this stepmom
I can't abide, and at that moment stepmother
Called for her Ashgirl to give her a kiss
To confuse her, to say she admired
Her frame, skinny as a rebar stick, she joked,
Then commanded her to spit-shine
The gentle-flush toilet bowl, "I want
That vitreous china to shine so brightly
No one would suspect it's made of clay!"
And Cinderella thought, when will I shine
Without perspiring, when will America
Come to me? And as she waited,
The culture troops marched forward, for her.

Preparation

In my earliest memory, I am in the womb still listening
To my brothers whisper I am too young to join them, or play

Horse, or wire ball in the street, or stretch with the long knives.
"You don't even know a road from a heated engine."

"But I know this wire of cord, these rose walls, the dead
Man's float," and they, long limbed, run off without me. I hear

My sisters say, "If you are a girl, here is the iron, this
Is a dishcloth, listen, this is a cramp and pad, get the wax

Out of your ears." "I will set the table for milk, I will
Warm the water, I will hear two sides of the heart at once."

They descend to the basement to fold. And my father prays,
"Until you can kneel on stone and beg, ashamed, for forgiveness

You are not worthy." "I can bow my head and hold it
In my hands for a moment, feeling the weight of the womb

On me. Is that sufficient unto you?" He is lost in devout prayer.
And my mother: "I am too old to hold you, you are eating

My spine, you will abandon me and leave me bereft
Once this water breaks; pray God, my last, it breaks soon.

These pains I have offered for the souls in Purgatory, my love."
"To honor you I shall leave now, just follow the stream

And arrive where I was elected to be, a small passage, eye
Of the needle, and feel the enormous light, I hope, of your world."

Andromache, on the Last Day of Mourning for Her Husband Hector

Robert Cooperman

Until I saw the pyre's flames licking you
like a great, hungry cat, I truly thought
you'd stand up from your blazing, oil soaked bed
and walk down to me and Astayanax,
that we'd stroll away from Troy's charnel house,
and find some quiet hinterland cottage
to live out our contented days, watching
our son grow to be a peaceful shepherd,
safe from court intrigues and eternal war.

I'd tend our garden, you'd cultivate grapes.
In Time's kindness we'd be joined by our son's
sweet wife, then grandchildren to whom you'd give
horse rides on your knees, while they'd shriek delight.
We'd fall asleep after our good day's work:
me with a needle and wool in my hands,
you mending a sandal: "No sense in waste,"
you'd say, not like a royal prince of Troy.

The fancy was so sweet I'd closed my eyes
to see and enjoy its balm more clearly:

beholding our lives, our deaths zephyr-serene:
changed into a pair of immortal doves
or twining trees, together forever.
I opened my eyes, expecting to see
that placid meadow of our grazing flocks.

But your pyre crackled, tears gouged down my face;
without thinking, I drew my viper blade,
to make the red slice and join you in death.
But that meddler Paris stopped my knife thrust.
I beat his chest with my fists, tried to scratch
his eyes out, but others dragged me away,
when all I wanted was to be with you.

Chimes

James B. Nicola

No chimes, no choir, no mourning rites;
No marble twelve feet tall;
For me they'll merely dim the lights
And silence may be all:

Or strike a rusted, tongueless bell
And crack it when I'm dead.
The pearly gates part just as well—
Better, some have said.

Interpretation

The Reverend Doctor hurled his epithets
like fire and brimstone from the very throne
of heaven, over all of us, his "pets,"
reminding us that we were not alone,

but being watched. One day he brought a book
with His picture in it to Thommie Meeks
(who rarely went to church) and made him look.
He'd dropped by Thommie's, Saturdays, for weeks.

Meeks was an orphan and a little slow,
but functional. His dad had been a friend
of Doctor Loud's. But Thommie didn't know
Loud's interest had a metaphysical end.

Next week the Doctor bought the boy a tie
and taught him how to tie all afternoon
while telling him over and over a whitish lie
to scare him: that he'd meet his Maker soon.

The note: "I'll be there Sunday, Rev. Loud.
Signed, Thommie Meeks. P. S. You see I tied

the thing myself. Thanks. Father will be proud."
Officials called the case a suicide.

At Thommie's services a tiny crowd
showed up: the Doctor, me, and an aunt, who cried.

Hide-and-Seek

Patrick Hicks

Sometimes, when you're sleeping,
and the furnace purrs against winter,
I wonder if we did the right thing,
taking you away from Korea.

At the heart of every adoption
is a ripping, a knifepoint, a breaking apart,
              like cracking open an oyster.

When you snore at midnight,
I think of your other possible lives
with a family in Stockholm or London.
You could have been raised near the sea,
or at the foot of a volcano.

But instead, you got us.

Did we do the right thing,
importing you to the other side of the world,
bringing you to the prairie and the ice?

As your bones push into the future,
and the netting of your heart widens,
you will jigsaw these truths into a mirror.

Your family past, so unknown, will make you
feel snapped. Broken.

Exiled.

But until then, I have to tell you
how much I love playing hide-and-seek,
how you run into a bedroom, looking
for me under a quilt,

in a wardrobe,

how you peek into a closet,
searching here and there for your father.

And when you find me,
it is like a lock clicking open.

Today, the truth is just child's play—
all you have to do is count to ten,
and open your eyes.

"Again," you shout. "Again!"

And so I hide. I wait in the dark,
like an easy answer.

The Earliest Hour

Jane Stuart

An unformed hour that melts away
Before the sun has set
Cannot come back until the night fades
And morning's unheard songs
Fill with hours that fill today
And moments we have met
In daylight groves,
And evening shades,
Where unborn time belongs.

Clogs

Noel Conneely

Norway pine
in winter snow
falls to the axeman.

Lumber worker
coughs up
to the company store.

Lean cattle quiver
on the brown plain
down in Spain.

A Basque lover,
dye under his nails,
folds his lady's hair.

South of Panama,
a child rocks itself to sleep,
beneath the rubber tree's shade.

Clogs

Clogs are handy;
slip them on,
no laces.

Bushy Park, Late October

A beech in late sun
turns nut brown, gold.
Tracing each letter
on the season's page.

A quick sally of birds
slices the wind.
They trumpet their song
on wingspan hill.

A boy with his father
pushes Columbus out
In a paper boat
on the duck pond.

Winter coughs
in a winter stream.
The whole spent season
going to seed.

At the Top of the House

Olivia Parkes

Outside, the postman is sprawling cigarette smoke across the front steps. A brief lawn stretches beyond the stairs and hellebores shelter in beds that abut the brick. The building is identical on each of its six floors. A lean woman presses out of the main entrance and dispels the haze, carrying a toddler and trailing two older boys. Without halting she says, "I wouldn't like to wait to hear from you. Is it you that leaves butts on the steps? You're to leave the letters, and not the butts. There's enough to clean up as it is."

In the flat upstairs at the top of the house an old woman pores over the weekend paper. The words appear to her magnified twice, by the round glass she ranges slowly over the page, and by the thick lenses of her spectacles. She reads deliberately and scrutinizes each article and advertisement.

Brunsworth House was built to last. It has been much the same since it was first erected, and for the thirty-three years Frances Mossor has spent there. The flats below have changed hands many times over the course of her tenancy. Now the other residents are young, downstairs, and busy. They fill the house with new furniture, children, dogs. From the sitting room window Frances sees them bustling in and out as she used to, dull green doors swinging shut behind them. There are none living here now who knew her then. Only Louise from the ground floor comes, on Sundays. For a small wage paid out of an envelope kept in a soup pot under the kitchen sink, she wipes the gathered dust and scans the expiry dates in the fridge. It has been this way for several years.

Louise is slight, mousy and whippet thin, though she has borne three sons. Surveying the faint mug rings that pattern the table, she tidies the vast afternoon away. Later, she will check upstairs to see that the milk is fresh, that nothing basic is needed. The help she gives the old woman is no bother to her. Their relationship is comfortable, for it does not challenge the assumption that they are strangers.

Their building is resolute, a block facing the street. Louise feels this staunch orientation at the top of each landing, as her body turns to the window to face a parallel row of terraced houses. She arrives slightly out of breath, scraping her feet at the doormat. Louise pushes aside the brass escutcheon and jostles the key in the lock until it swings once around, cleanly. She enters to silence and unstirred air. Peering first into the empty kitchenette, she follows the narrow hall into the sitting room, calling once, "Mrs. Mossor." The room is spare and well kept, its few dated furnishings standing heavily at rest. The cushions on the low sofa that dominates the space are dented. Louise often finds the old woman resting here, her head thrown back, limbs thoughtlessly arranged about the body bunched like pillow stuffing under the folds of her dress. The sofa faces a tiled fireplace, its grate boarded up and painted.

It is here that she finds her. Louise thinks first that it is only a garment, a white nightdress, crumpled in front of the hearth. The quiet is awash with the radiator's persistent hiss. There is something in the nightdress.

Last year they had mice. Louise loaded the traps and put them in bin liners when they were full. Though she never touched them the grey bellies had seemed very soft. The form here looks soft too, like a crab dead on a beach, its shell yielding after hours in the sun.

Frances moved into the top of the house after her divorce, and before parking spaces replaced the lawn at the back of the building. Her taxi waited at the front while she swung through the front doors three times, carrying her things to the sixth floor. At sixty she had been young by comparison; she found the other residents all at least ten years older than her.

The woman just below her, Frances thought *really* old. But she trotted anyway up and down the stairs, smelling of cheap alcohol and boasting; she had children, once a week they would come in a car and take her to dinner. One day they didn't bring her back. The daughter came later and packed a valise that followed her to the nursing home. And the elderly gentleman in number Four; he fell against his bath and had to be moved to the ground flat, where he died. But really, she did not have much to do with any of them, because she was out. Every day there was reason to go somewhere. She needs fresh bread, furniture polish, or a color rinse. For these amenities, and even to dry clean her winter coat, Frances traveled to Durand Park, an adjacent suburb with lawns that didn't dry out in the summer and a high street lively with women in pressed dresses.

The grocery there, Frances remembers, her glass ranging over the day's news, was splendid. Pyramids of bright fruits yielded to a long white delicatessen counter flanked by two bakery stands. The larger was laden with bread. Below the counter glass, a generous spread of meats and cheeses. And on the countertop a handsome roast always presided. Behind all this, a rack of spitted chickens turning and browning.

Sometimes she would buy a rotisserie, and eat it over two days. Then set the carcass boiling.

The memory of this place rearranges itself continuously but recalls no particular scene. It adheres briefly around shapes, colors, smells, without incident. Ruddy hands busy themselves behind the counter, fat drips liquid gold from the turning chickens.

Other parts are preserved differently. These memories are cool, distinct. She looks in on them as though through a window, into rooms she has lived in but cannot re-enter. These are her visits to Marconette's, the jeweler in Durand Park.

At a glance Marconette was only a woman, unremarkable though attractive: fortyish, the slight solidity about her waist mediated by a pair of unscuffed heels. But Frances can still see those hands resting on the glass case, weighted with rings, the nails gleaming like garnets.

The first time, Frances is brought to the shop by a trifle. An earring-back had skittered down the bathroom sink. There are no other customers. Frances notices that the woman at the till is wearing very expensive jewelry. Her coiffed hair is bleached almost to white. Something in her aspect seems to necessitate a compliment, and Frances settles like a honeybee on several features before praising a brooch pinned to the younger woman's blazer, opals set in a constellation of flowers spilling from a basket of woven silver. "That silver pin—it's splendid." With the gentleness of the admonishment—*platinum*—Frances registers the smoothness of Marconette's countenance, the perfect arches of her eyebrows as bold as her precise, red mouth. "Yes, a gift. From my husband." The husband: it was his shop, but his wife was always at the front of it. His occasional appearances inspired in Frances an observant courtesy, but she preferred the shop empty of anyone but herself and Marconette.

With each encounter, the jeweler's satisfaction became more apparent. Her composure is impenetrable, lacquered, and Frances attributes it to some infallible sense of the cost and value of things. Frances returns to the shop many times, as the sea swells to meet a monstrous and indifferent moon.

This woman's pleasure seemed unassailable, guarded by the lapdog at the door, her husband, and the two sons mentioned in a passing way that asserted both independence and affection. It was this happiness that Frances treated with deference, as something not to be envied, but revered. She goes to Marconette's as if to warm her hands by the blue, irradiating warmth of an electric fire, where nothing ever turns to ash.

After her first visit Frances finds that she must drop in with greater regularity. Initially she comes only for a little mending. She brings a broken chain, a tarnished silver cigarette case that needs cleaning. She even takes a beaded purse from her youth with a kink in its fine brass zip, to see if Marconette might make the seam run smoothly again. When there is no longer any need for mending, Frances begins to buy trinkets, little baubles.

She enjoys the conversations that envelop these transactions, their conspiratorial tone of appraisal. The jeweler's cool presence seems able to blow upon desire, red-hot, and fix it permanently in its pleasing shape. At Marconette's, the beauty of a thing might never prove cause for regret. Here it is as if happiness itself, like any jewel, might be held to the light under an expert eye and purchased for a reasonable price. The display case is always between them.

For a long time these purchases are meagre, affordable. Only on one occasion does Frances spend much more than she can spare. She enters to find Marconette engaged with another customer. The doorbell rankles the air in the room, pulled taut between them. The woman at the counter wears an oversized mac, though it is not raining outside. She seems drab and harried, out of place in the jewelry shop. Frances busies herself with a case of rings and listens. "I'm sorry," Marconette repeats, "but I'm quite sure. All glass. It has," she pauses, "no value." She lifts a white hand and holds it open, as if to demonstrate that it is empty. With the other she pushes a glinting mass towards the customer without removing her fingers. Frances doesn't catch the stranger's reply but hears Marconette yielding, making an offer, *though we do not usually deal in costume jewelry.* As the other woman leaves, Frances sees that she is older than she thought. Two spots of color stand high in her unmade face, as though her cheeks have been rudely pinched. The necklace had been precious until now, Frances supposes. She did not like to see it. A beautiful thing shamed under strained circumstances. To see its glamour exchanged for pennies.

The voice Marconette greets Frances with is as hard and brilliant as a diamond. Her composure seems greater than ever. She smiles, baring teeth that are surprisingly small, round, very even. It seems to Frances that something more is now required of her. In the face of this transaction, and the high red points of the other woman's face. "The day is particularly fine," Frances ventures. "And I should like something that does it justice." The response comes without hesitation. "A necklace," Marconette suggests, her smile turning up as though to conjure, between her lips, a string of pearls. Her own neck today is bare. It is so white it is almost bloodless. She continues, "These are new. Every woman should have a set, don't you think?" The pearls are plump, nestled close in a single strand. Frances is alarmed by the swiftness of this injunction, delivered so closely to that verdict: it has, *no value.* The words arrive like a challenge.

Though she makes a show of trying them on, Frances knows that she will buy the pearls. That she must. That to escape this air of disappointment untarnished, she must demonstrate her appreciation for beauty, and for things that last. The price is such that she must pay in installments. These she sends by post, for this is the last visit she makes to Marconette's.

On the bus ride home Frances sees a group of men erecting an enormous Christmas tree, naked, in the center of the green. She remembers the pleasure she took as a child, warm in the parlor, fettering pine boughs in handmade paper chains.

The final installment owed for the pearl necklace is never paid. Her seventh cheque returns undelivered. In this way Frances learns that the shop has closed. The couple left in a hurry. A dry cleaner takes over the premises and rumors circulate in the local press. There are allegations of chicanery, a racket. Claims crop up like weeds, over fraudulent appraisals, lucite gems and composites, stones set in foil. A man has married his wife with a synthetic diamond. Frances does not listen to gossip.

Alone at the top of the house, Frances grows old like those before her. Time winds her bones more tightly, coiling her spine towards the ground. There is less cause to venture to the Durand Park grocery, and she restricts her journeys to the local shops. On a summer afternoon, groping with her cane along the brief stretch home from the corner store, a boy in a striped shirt stops her. He is perhaps twelve. "Look," he says. "I've lost it. My kite, lost. Up there," he says. "It's up there," straightening his arm and forefinger above him. Frances looks up from the mustardy smear of catkins on the pavement. It is a labor to unbend. She moves methodically, tilting first her head to one side, in order to hinge her neck back and raise her eyes. She has not looked at the sky like this for a long time. It is cloudless, utterly blue. And then like a bell being struck a bird breaks, skating across the glassy azure: a marvel. She watches transfixed until it has flown her vision and the sky hangs empty as before, a void without time or movement. When again she faces the street the boy too has gone.

At home she finds he has taken the purse from her handbag. After this, her visits even to the local shops become intermittent. Without their former regularity, these places seem remote, then unknown. By means of a spidery note pinned to the front door, Louise is engaged to provide her weekly services.

The future settles round her ankles and Frances dwells often in the past. Though she feels perhaps a distant fascination that the events of her life have cohered into a story, nearly complete, Frances does not linger on the forces that have driven it here. The slate has been cleared many times. War and emigration dismantled the first beginning, when she wore a navy school uniform, and lived in her mother's house. A new life was undone by a pair of stillborns in the kitchen sink, the divorce. But it is not narrative that interests her now. Her mind instead plays over the routines of the last thirty years alone at Brunsworth House, like variations on a theme, as in the music favored by the classical station the radio has been tuned to for a decade. The period of her tenancy here seems somehow boundless, the years free from either expectation or regret. She doesn't linger on the life; that was not hers to determine. Recollections pool instead around its living. They open onto the whiteness of a deli counter or the smell of broiling chickens. And she is not unhappy. It is neither happiness nor unhappiness. Only an equanimity of spirit.

The frosted glass on the front door darkens briefly and the morning post shunts through the mail slot. When letters arrive Frances does not open them at once. She reads the envelopes first, scrutinizing even the postmark with her magnifying glass. She treats all the delivered material with the same impartial consideration. Bending over a take-away menu she reads 'Szechuan chicken' and files it with the others on the mantle behind a brass clock. Next to this sits a battered chocolate tin embossed with a young woman's face, flirtatiously tilted, a smile that shows her teeth. Inessential items gather inside with pins and spare buttons, safe where they may be forgotten and not lost. The room is tidy, as neat and dry as the old woman's body. The only irregularity is a cracked line in the plaster and paint that encircles the top of the room. A building fault leads to a recurring fissure that begins in the far corner and creeps slowly around. In the first two decades of life there Frances periodically had the crack filled and the wall repainted. It has been years since she has bothered and the crawling line has come full circle, reaching round to its origin.

Frances sits at the table and plays Patience. The fissure circling the walls makes the room look like an egg that a giant has cracked with his spoon. If such a creature, poised outside, threatened suddenly to take her from this place, she would not even then look up from the descending tableaux that she is building, of hearts, of Jacks, of Kings.

Evening draws and closes. A blue light flickering in the window at the top of the house goes out. As the television set darkens a white seam glows briefly in the center before the screen blinks shut. The evening programmes have covered the preamble to the New Year, and the gap between the hands of the mantle clock narrows toward the hour of celebration. Below, someone is having a party. A steady bass thumps through the floorboards and occasional shrieks puncture the night outside. None of these noises reaches Frances, for whom the texture of sound has thickened to resemble felt.

There are nights now when the old woman is so tired that she does not change into her loose white nightdress. This evening, she struggles into it and swallows a ritual sleeping pill. As she turns out the lamp the sitting room window ignites. The sky is riotous, the black showered with streaks of light. She approaches the window and stands with her hands on the ledge, watching the fireworks, framed by the heavy parted drapes. The gauzy inner curtain hangs over her back like a veil or a shroud, and her face is the same papery white as the night-dress. She watches until the last sparks peter out, and then the night is dark again.

In a corner window at the top of Brunsworth House a little specter vanishes from sight. Frances turns to make her way to bed and the room she faces is bitumen black. But the way is well worn. She steps away from the windowsill cautiously though without trepida-tion. Gingerly she treads a practiced diagonal towards the dark, famil-iar hall. There is only one turn to make, into the corridor that leads to the bedroom. When she raises her hand to brace herself briefly inside the doorframe she pushes instead against empty air. Somewhere along the way a step has been miscounted. Her outstretched arm disrupts her balance and her weight spins away from her into the dark.

The fear of falling is constant. After all her years it is no longer the fall Frances fears, but only the inability to rise. Falling she thinks *once I have fallen I cannot get up* and sees a clear blue field, interrupt-ed briefly by the passage of something winged and far away. It is dark when she opens her eyes. The pill draws her heavily into the carpet. She is conscious of the need to get to the settee, to raise herself. Crawling, asleep for a moment, then crawling. The lights are out. Why does it matter where you make your bed if all is dark? It is not so undignified, really, there will be no one in the morning to see her, to know that she has not managed tonight to put herself to bed. The room is still and the risen moon bathes the pavements outside. Sometime in the night a final glancing light drawing shadows from the walls goes out, and then the darkness is entire.

Louise stands over the bundled body on the floor. Something must be done. What a horrid thing. Not her, of course, but someone must. Must hide it away. The eyes are faintly open, pale and opaque. Louise flushes dully, as though she has been caught at something. It is just this, after all, from which she is hiding. She is hiding her children from it, and her time. Of her time she is perhaps the most afraid. Louise retrieves a clean tea towel from the kitchen and her hand shivers over the dead face to cover it. She straightens up and steps back, facing the fireplace. A sheaf of letters rests in neatly knifed envelopes behind a heavy mantle clock. A woman's face smiles up from the gold tin next to it. Unobserved, Louise lifts the lid. There's nothing much here: a comb with a broken tooth, expired train tickets and some loose buttons. She shuffles the bric-a-brac about with her fingers and dislodges, to a dawning surprise, something precious. She holds them up. It's lovely, the way they catch and reflect the light. Louise has always liked pearls, so hard and lustrous. Her mother wore them. Impervious, like all things beautiful.

A tremor in the winter light brightens the room. The necklace gleams and Louise too is illuminated. Standing at the top of the house with the pearls held out and the bundle at her feet, Louise does not think of death. Instead she desires: another's happiness, beauty, a string of pearls. These have been made in shallow, brackish beds where the oysters are busy, licking their wounds. Louise looks out at the row of terraced houses across the street. Veiled windows, staring like witnesses. Without another thought she slips the necklace in the pocket at the front of her dress.

It occurs then to Louise with something like pleasure, that she will have a story to tell. That something has happened to her. She will be Queen of the House. Indeed, her astonishment at the gravity of the moment is such that she cannot bear to dial the appropriate number. For the medics rushing up those stairs, past the sets of twinned doors, unseeing, will give away the ending without any exposition. Better, tomorrow perhaps, to encounter a neighbor on the stairs, and to relate a discovery made only an instant ago. To express the fresh horror of the moment, and impart it to another. Descending the stairs to her own apartment, she rubs the beads in her pocket, passing down the strand from one to the other, as though they are prayers.

Father-Daughter Reunion

John Grey

After twenty years,
he wasn't up for small talk,
just "God, how lovely you've grown"
and "Would you like a beer?"

He'd done the walking out.
She was the tracker.
Not much of a place.
He lived there alone.

"You look just like your mother/'
he told her.
He unscrewed his bottle.
Her fingers roamed the neck of hers.

Ten years before,
she'd have smashed it over his head -
for the tears on the school bus,
for the bruise on her mother's arm.

But forgiveness had grown beautiful,
regret had gotten old.

In twenty years, they'd both grown a thirst.

Her, two beers worth.

Put him down for four.

This Winter Crop

Winter is the rack, the auto-da-fe.
In December cruelty, roots battle
to the death of the flowers above
for their place in frozen soil.
In my cellar, the ones that made
it out in time hunker down in the dark:
the hanging garlic, sacks of carrots
and potatoes, boxes of apples.
My sweat was a rescue mission.
Now it's a bulwark against
the north-west, its winds,
its stranglehold of cold,
the snow that smothers,
leaves no green to chance.
Stoking the wood stove,
I make my promise to the earth below.
Sipping cider, I celebrate
our shared dark humor.
I am Lazarus with three days growth
and a wobbly knee.
The ground is a wounded deer
hiding from the hunter.

Buying Rice

Darrell Dela Cruz

Two ladies cover their heads
with red umbrellas. Their golden
dresses dry, but the elephants
they stand on wait in the small shade.

A golden bowl hovers
over a kingdom.
Filled with cooked rice.

Three ladies: one
a Bodhisattva displaying
her crown carries a wedge.
A halo around the second,
the pattern of loti all over
her dress. A single exposed
shoulder on the last, a bud
woven in her hair.
All their faces have no detail.

A butterfly: the body black,
the antennae red. A large triangle

which replaces the abdomen is yellow—
the same color as the wings.

Buddha on the side,
away from the 22 villagers.
Some split the grains.
Some dance with the white
chickens. One man
eyes a woman's breast. The others
tend the field.

A blue pheasant in mid
flight, wings stretched to soar
or fly away. A trinket,
a rabbits foot, dangles
from the mouth.
All stationary.

Two female dignitaries
with their palms up
as to beg or persuade.
Above them a dragonfly
encased in a yellow prison

Ascent

Michael D. Riley

Grandma drifts noiselessly away
in the ancient hot air balloon
she found on a postcard yesterday:
bright copper guy wires, white Victorian
Easter basket, colored sheeting
hand-stitched in quilted rows
around a plaque painted
with her name, all of it rippling
around the superheated air.

It has been a long time
already since the squares of land
far below held a neighbor's name,
spires or bells a promise.
But the air is pure,
sun and moon next door.

Her hands upon the basket rails
shake with every tremor,
but she has grown light
in the lighter air: shallow breathing,
tiny meals, fitful sleep.

When the anchor rope first fell away
she feared the loss of everything below,
only to find it takes this long
to gather lift enough to catch
the graceful curve of earth, and room
enough to let it go.

Early Pictures: With Ed

I still love the lie of photographs,
>their steely quiet, their close embrace
of the light. The way intention
>with its scissors trims one precise
square of someone's life, and holds it there.

They hold on so nobly, hopelessly
>to the odd-shaped eyeglasses,
shirts and pants with impossible collars
>and cuffs, people smaller than their lives.
I pity them, these failing witnesses,

5 by 7 hands grasping the river
>of developer and stop-bath, as we did
in our Summer of Photography, diving
>into the renewed world behind our
two-dollar mail-order glass eyes.

We found infinite shades of gray, geometry
>instead of simplicity, framed

ether, the pilgrim's progress thumb-tacked
       to the cardboard, her smile off-center,
refusing still everything we hoped for.

Variables

Christine DeSimone

When we argued we were
like surgeons, our blades looking
for the right seam. We tore our most
important pieces and then began
to patch: even Cepheid stars
pulse with a heartbeat because

they are dying. You reminded me often
that nothing lasts. But I believe
every ending is a newness:
every atom we've possessed passed
through suns and souls on its way
to us, belonging first to Beethoven

or Joan of Arc, or the vein of a leaf,
or a drop of dew. You will trudge
home from the Plaza d'Italie
to your tiny Parisian dorm
in a three-euro scarf, the light snowfall
crunching into craters under your boots.

It is the same journey:
In another hemisphere called California,
I will load groceries into my car,
and the palsied bagboy will wish me
a nice day, one hand twisted
helplessly to his side.

When exactly did we part?
This soggy spring is a mange of gray
and the sky is inconsolable,
throbbing with the dense dim
rhythm of a once bright star.

The Alder and I

John Sibley Williams

The alder and I share a mother.
Unseen, she expands below
the length of our outstretched arms.
Each time we discover sustenance elsewhere,
it seems to trace back to that first seed.
Each time we turn our backs to her voice,
she pushes forth another inch
from the surface soil.

The alder and I share a father.
Impenetrable, we are a testimony
to prodigy and blood.
When lighting gathers in frantic reds
between our arms
and releases,
falling the branches around us,
we realize how "home"
both creates and destroys us,
that we'll always be planted
too near the house.

The alder and I share a ghost.

He's within the glass that separates us

from clawing at each other's faces.

We must suffice for a mutual disturbing of dreams.

He's always looking in (and out),

selecting just the right void to speak from.

This morning we're both reminded

of our flightlessness.

Tonight, perhaps, we'll forget we're not clouds

or brothers.

Bearings

The moon plummets
unnoticed
into the ocean,
its stars taking root
as easily
in the sandy bed
below.

When I press my ear to the sky now: the hollow of an absent body.
When I press my heart to the water: eternity played on the same flat
    key.

Seagulls chase nourishment
around planets and islands.
My dreams now bound
in kelp and current,
the cloud-lining of whales.
Still I am no closer to meaning.

In the firmament's collapse,
only the metaphor has changed:
from comet to ship, both

search vainly
for a compass
fallen overboard.

Bridal Veil

Matt Schumacher

Someone names a small town
after a waterfall since
its delicate trail of mist
looks like a bridal veil.
A ghost town's history
ensues: Larch Mountain pine
falls down a log flume to
the disappearing Palmer sawmill.
Lumber boom families
perish due to smallpox
and diphtheria epidemics.
The trust for public land destroys
the last standing buildings,
except for the cemetery,
but thankfully, there's more
to the metaphor: the air wears vapor
like a layered dress.
all is defined by a shining finery of rain,
and a tiny post office rests
by the highway like
a clapboard chapel of true happiness.
Thousands of brides and grooms

briefly stay, in spring and summer,
soon on the way to honeymoons.
They send guests wedding invitations
bearing Bridal Veil's insignia of bliss:
its postmark like a goodbye kiss
from a forgotten town.

Crater Lake Ode

You'll never view blue this unearthly
unless you peruse its depths in person.
Such blue mystifies the eye
from rhapsodizing iris
to stupefied pupil,
immerses tourist
and glowing oceanographer.
No one can map the place
Crater Lake's blue takes you.
Shades this deep must be trapped
for centuries inside collapse,
in shadows cast by blown volcano dome,
and slowly released each season,
through melting ice and blizzards
that encastle Wizard Island's pine spires,
as if, with open eye,
the earth were dreaming.

Barbed Wire Fence Museum

Ted Lardner

1.

The house breathes. The draft runs up the nape of the stairs, saws a cut-away into the attic. The opposite of yoga is cocaine. By June 9 or 10, summer roadside roses are blooming and the daisies that run wild on the disturbed ground are the first, best shot of the heat spell that right now is breaking on the knee of a *derecho*. This morning I watched the first effects. Wind lifted and lowered the branches of the copper beech and my wife, my beloved, enfurled in dreams beside me, tensing.

2.

We should not carry anger in our thoughts like wicker baskets of barbed wire in our hands. The weather? It's already turning. Its song is all swerve. When you get down the trail, yes, you can hear yourself think think think, true, but then what have you got? Who is that, talking nonsense into your ear? It's like this: When she said, "I want you to be happy," and he felt it like a shock, a kick in the heart, his right hand still enclosed the muscle memory of her left.

3.

He rides shotgun. What else can he do. I make him listen and he makes me listen, our own music on a station from back home where we both were alive. "I'm listening," I say to him and to the light after weeks and weeks of rain. He looks through the window. I've parked and sit now, waiting until he asks, "What's that?" of a catbird, talking to angels, which are other catbirds, each in its thorn bush, at the genetic level, listening to every other catbird's song.

4.
One room holds a display of lightning.
One room, a display of oceanic silences.
One room—"Sadness"—holds sadnesses from around the world,
organized by hemispheres.
One room holds a catbird,
one room, a western meadowlark,
and one, a wall of machetes.
One room no one goes into.

5.
In the afterlife my father crawls through storm clouds pursued by
        lightning.
In this life my mother becomes a teasel-burr of thunder, from a stem
        on a cut bank
next to a parking lot hanging, decorated Tuesday by lightning, yet on
        Wednesday
a barbed wire fence.

Thunder

I lay instead beside her, listening.
It was as though a family
traveled across our sky.
What is solid? What lasts?
Aunts, cousins. Conversations
inside clouds. What could they see,
daylight in every direction,
impenetrably bright?
A book she is reading
speaks of a world overlying this one.
This house, she'd explained, would be, like, a castle.
Invisible to us. But here.
In the dark after bedtime,
on the step of the porch, a man sat, playing scales.
I almost got up to go see him.

Mar 20 Flow Studio, Cleveland Yoga

Mom said, "It's the first day of spring."
Helen said, "I took four Motrins."
Toby (the puppy) said, "Smell this!"
Pete (the brother) said, "It's just like
Imperial Japan. It is in the water
And it goes into their heads."
Rush Limbaugh said, "Prostitute, slut."
Pete (the father) said, "with the kids gone…"
and then he stared into the bonfire.
The bonfire said, "Nothing lasts."
The bonfire said, "I am a whirlwind in the ground."
The creek said, "Upstream is heaven."
The peepers said, "Pee-pee, pee-pee."
A mosquito on the screen said,
"I am the first and the last."

Alphabet of My Grandmother

Elana Zaiman

Adventure of 1997

A white-haired woman smiles the excited smile of a toddler as a young man sets a motorcycle helmet on her head, boosts her onto his bike, and drives her up, down, and around the back roads of New Paltz, New York. She is wearing a cotton jersey, a cotton skirt, a slip, a girdle, Peds, and beige orthopedic shoes. I am not there. But I know this is the outfit she is wearing, because this is the outfit she always wears. I know this woman's outer clothes and I know her underclothes and I know her smell and I know her laughter and I know her likes and I know her dislikes and I know her expressions like I know myself. Maybe better.

This eighty-four-year old woman, this daredevil, this Evel Knievel, is my grandmother.

The young man on the motorcycle is her grandson, my cousin Noah. Upon their safe return, Noah says to his father, "I've never been so scared in my life."

Brain Not Working

In April 2005 I visit my grandmother in her New Rochelle condo with my four-year old son Gabriel. We are eating lunch in her kitchen with Moira, her weekday caregiver. My grandmother is sitting in her wheelchair. She is wearing a knit scoop neck, black, white, and beige, and a beige skirt. She has lost weight since last I saw her. Her face has thinned, and her body has diminished, and her skirt sits on her funny, the two front pockets off kilter.

My grandmother holds a fork in her right hand and she pushes egg salad onto the fork with her left forefinger. She leans over her plate and she lifts the forkful of egg salad to her mouth. She pauses. She stares at the forkful of egg salad as if she is trying to remember what to do with it. She pauses again. She eats.

My grandmother doesn't remember Gabriel. I'm not sure she remembers me. She stares at me as if she is straining to see through a dense fog. She closes her eyes and she falls asleep. Her head drops onto her chest. We wake her to finish eating.

Gabriel talks to her as if he's the grown-up, and she's the child. He enunciates his words and he raises his voice so she can hear. "We're going to Baltimore," he says. "And you're staying here."

During lunch, Moira asks my grandmother how she's feeling.

My grandmother says, "My brain's not working."

Cucumbers

When my sister Sarina was twelve and I fifteen, we convinced our six-ty-five-year old grandmother to take us to the movie *Animal House*.

"Are you sure it's appropriate?" my grandmother asked.

"Sure, we're sure," we said. The movie was rated R.

My grandmother raised her eyebrows, but carted us to the theater anyway. Side-by-side we sat, the three of us, munching popcorn, sucking the chocolate off Raisinets, and laughing as we watched the Faber college frat boys, Otter and John and Flounder and Pinto and Boon drink six-packs of beer, and sneak glimpses of half-naked women. Their language: gazongas, bastards, buns, fuck, assholes, tits, horseshit.

One of many memorable scenes takes place in the local super-market when Otter says to an older woman standing in front of the cucumber bin, "Mine's bigger." The woman (who we later learn is his Dean's wife) glances at him, a playful glint in her eyes. "My cucumber," says Otter. "It's bigger."

On our way out of the theatre, my grandmother turned to us and said, "What a silly movie. I didn't understand a thing."

Sarina and I giggled.

That evening when we stood in my grandmother's Scarsdale kitchen preparing dinner, Sarina opened the refrigerator, pulled out a foot long cucumber, and said, "Mine's bigger."

My grandmother laughed and laughed. "You girls. You understood!"

Danced Her Last Dance

My grandmother was known by her great granddaughters as "Hokey Pokey Grandma." She would hold her hands near her head, elbows protruding forward, wiggle her forefingers in the air, clack her tongue, spin around, and sing, "You do the Hokey Pokey and you turn yourself around..." Her great granddaughters would mimic her and they would whirl around and around her living room until they tired of dizziness. That was when my grandmother could stand. When she could turn herself around without falling. When she could sing. When she could speak. When she had her wits about her.

My grandmother danced her last Hockey Pokey many years before she danced her last dance. Before she departed. Bit The Dust. Breathed her last breath. Perished. Passed away. Passed on. Circled the drain. Expired. Checked out. Coded. Croaked. Crossed over. Kicked the bucket. Went to a better place. Before she was gathered to her people. Was taken from us. Was laid to rest. Was called to a higher place. Was no more. Was gone. Went to meet her Maker. Went the way of all flesh. Went to heaven. Went to the great dugout in the sky. Left this life. Left us.

Enough with the euphemisms. I prefer to call it what it is. Died.

At 3:00 a.m. on April 3, 2009, my grandmother, Dorothy Florence Farber Shanok, died in her New Rochelle condo. She was ninety-six-and-a-half-years old. She had hoped to live to 100. She had hoped to receive a letter from the president. But that was when she was well enough to know what a letter was, what a president was, and who the president was.

Exasperating

My grandmother's self-deprecating comments like, "I'm no good at that."

Her loud noises.

Her "ohhs" and "ahhhs" and coughs and farts and burps and throat clearings. Noises that kept her company when she was alone. Noises that kept us company when we visited. Noises that said: Don't forget me. I'm here in this house even if you cannot see me.

Her nosiness.

As kids, when Sarina and I used to visit, she would rummage through our backpacks and duffel bags. We got her good. We wrote notes for her to find when she snooped. Notes like, "Hi Grams, we see you," and "Hey Grams, what are you doing here?"

Her comments about my short haircut, "It's too severe."

About my clothes, "Again with the dark green? The color drains you."

About the customer service at high-end department stores, in hearing distance of our saleswoman, "The help here is terrible."

About the lunch bills she would make me check three times to be sure she hadn't been short-changed, "You can never trust anybody."

About the way she would refer to her housekeepers and companions: Rosa, Hyacinth, Mercedes, Vena, and Teresa as, "what's her name."

About the way she would refer to African-Americans as *shvartz-as* (the black ones), *blondinas* (the blond ones), or coloreds. I knew her attitude had a lot to do with how she was raised, that she was told to be wary of black people, but that she never re-evaluated this teaching bothered me. "Grams," I'd say. "Please don't say those words. They're derogatory." Her reaction. A narrowing of the eyes. A tightening of the lips. Like a reprimanded child. For a moment, she was silenced. But only for a moment.

How could I love this woman so much?

Farberware

My grandmother grew up in the home of Simon and Ella Farber, Russian immigrants from the town of Antopol. She was the youngest of four children: Isidor, Milton, Estelle, and then Dorothy, my grandmother. She was born on September 26, 1912, at 246 South Ninth Street in Brooklyn.

My grandmother admired her older sister, Estelle, to whom she felt she could never compare. Estelle was beautiful. Estelle was smart. Estelle was a student. Estelle was a college graduate. Estelle was a poet. Estelle was everything my grandmother wasn't. At least according to my grandmother. According to my mother: Estelle was a lousy housekeeper, a space cadet, and not as beautiful as her mother, my grandmother.

My grandmother's father, Simon, was an inventor. He invented the Adjusto-Lite (a light that clamped onto a bed board to make reading in bed easier on the eyes). He invented the first electric coffee per-colator. He manufactured aluminum-clad stainless steel cooking ware, hammered aluminum giftware, chromium plate giftware, electric coffee makers, coffee robots, broiler robots, candy dishes, planters, spit-toons, lazy susans, pots, pans, and umbrella stands under the label: Farberware.

My grandmother's mother, Ella, worked at the factory along-side her husband. When Ella and Simon decided to marry, Ella said to him, "We get married and you buy your partner out. I'm your partner now." And she was. His life partner, his business partner, his equal.

My grandmother and her siblings were raised by their caretaker, Sarah, and their governess, Mrs. Walstrom. There was also the cook, and the chauffeur.

On February 4, 1936, at the age of twenty-four, my grand-mother married Hyman Shanok, and moved from her parents home in Brooklyn, New York to be with her husband, the lawyer, in Chicago, Illinois. Hyman had his eye on a judgeship, but because my grand-mother missed her family, they returned to New York, and he joined Farberware as the company lawyer.

My grandmother and grandfather had two children: my mother, Ann, born in 1937, and her brother, Charles, born in 1940. Though my grandmother never worked, she raised my mother and my uncle as she was raised, with nannies.

My grandmother would often speak about her father's inven-tions and her mother's ingenuity. She would regale me with tales about how her mother walked door-to-door to give away Farberware products, the only request of the woman-of-the-house, "Try it. If you like it, tell your friends." In this way, Farberware became a household name.

My grandmother was so proud of the Faberware label that whenever we ate in a restaurant or visited someone's home, she would turn over candy dishes and lift up hot water urns to show us the Farberware label. She could spot Farberware products miles away. About non-Farberware products she had this to say, "It's made of tissue paper and spit."

Gone

My grandmother was gone before she died. Not all the time. But she was gone for a good part of the last six years of her life. Mini-stroke after mini-stroke after mini-stroke left her in the fuzzy space between the world of the living and the world of the dead, and she went where her mind went, to the lapses between the synapses.

When she was ninety-one, when she could still speak, we had the following phone conversation:

Elana: Hey Grams.

Grandma: Hey honey, when will I see you?

Elana: You just did, Grams. I came by a few days ago.

Grandma: I guess I wasn't home.

Elana: But you were, Grams. I saw you.

Grandma: Oh.

Hearing Aids

Large beige hearing aids sat like deformed kidney beans in my grandmother's ears. Still, she had trouble hearing.

Elana: I'm sending you lots of love and hugs.

Grandma: You're setting me up at Robin's house?

Elana: I'm in Seattle.
Grandma: You're at the piano?

Elana: Did you take a walk today?
Grandma: Did I make some rocks today?

Elana: Do you want some more salad?
Grandma: Warm towels?

Elana: Grams, you need your hearing aid.
Grandma: I need to see a feeling agent?

When she was still present, though fading, and we, her family, were talking in her kitchen, dinning room, or living room, she would often slip her hearing aids out of her ears, place them on the table, or in her pocket and close her eyes.

Too much commotion. She needed peace.

Inventor of Tales
Like her father, Simon, my grandmother was an inventor. She didn't invent coffee percolators or Adjusto-Lite's. She invented tales. Tales about places and people and objects and events she knew little about.

When my mother was eight, and my uncle five, their mother, my grandmother, took them to Fort Tryon Park in Washington Heights. There they had a perfect view of The George Washington Bridge. My grandmother proceeded to explain the bridge's history, "George Washington was here on this side of the bridge with the Americans, and the English were on the other side of the bridge. The English wanted to attack the Americans by crossing The George Washington Bridge, but the Americans guarded the bridge so well, the English couldn't attack."

Her historical account made no sense. She was speaking of events that happened in the late 1700's. The George Washington Bridge didn't open until 1931.

Jewish Man Wanted
Seven years after my grandfather died, my mother and my uncle placed a classified ad in *The Jewish Monthly*.

> Refined widow, mid-70s. Our mother and grandmother would kill us if she knew we were doing this, but we want to introduce her to someone, who like her, is sincere, bright, funny, attractive, healthy, Jewishly-minded, financially secure, and wishing for companionship. Note about yourself, father or grandpa to Box 2078, Jewish Monthly, NY.

We received many replies. My uncle called one possible suitor and met him prior to introducing him to my grandmother. My Grandmother agreed to one date with this man, after which she was disgusted. "He's not Hy," she said. With these words, her dating days were over.

Kitchen
This is what I remember of my grandmother's kitchen.

Late nights eating Breyers chocolate, vanilla, and strawberry ice cream.

Cupboards with candy: Coffee Nibs, Nestle Crunch, Kit Kat, Krackel, Tic Tacs, Milky Ways, Mars, Mounds, licorice drops, and butterscotch. For *nashing* and nibbling and nudging into her purse pockets.

Homemade vegetarian kishka, the recipe on the back of a box of Tam Tams.

Homeade rugelach, *putchkies*, cinnamon buns. Usually slightly overdone. When I lived in Manhattan, she often sent me home with a bag of *putchkies*. I remember once walking on Broadway with my bag of *putchkies* and handing them over to a homeless man seated on the sidewalk. I kept on walking. Moments later I heard someone run up behind me. I turned to find the homeless man standing there with my grandmother's bag of *putchkies*. "I can't eat these," he said. "They're burnt."

Letters

"I have work to do," my grandmother would say. "Work," for my grandmother meant sitting in her study and sorting through her mail or going through her bills or writing checks for baby namings, bar or bat mitzvahs, birthdays, weddings, or anniversaries, or readying herself for the accountant, or writing thank-you notes or letters on cards from the MET or the Audubon Society. Before writing on a card, she would pen a rough draft in her flowery script on yellow legal pads or on the backs of envelopes. She had to get it right, not because she was a perfectionist, but because she was self-conscious about her lack of education, which concluded with a diploma from Erasmus Public High School in Brooklyn.

After she died, I searched for the pile of her letters I had saved over the years and I re-read them. What I remembered about her letters before I re-read them: her newsy, chatty, reporter-like style, and her lack of self-reflection. What I hadn't remembered were her more self-reflective and honest letters. Excerpts of two of these letters follow.

The first letter was written two months before her husband, Hyman, died. For many months his lungs filled with fluid and he had to hook himself up to an oxygen tank in his office. He spent the last few weeks of his seventy-four-years in New Rochelle Hospital struggling to breathe.

Sept 7, 1980
2:30 a.m. and cannot sleep
Elana Dear,

Many, many thanks for being so understanding and sympathetic. I did not show Grandpa your letter. I told him it was for me. I didn't want him to know how worried everyone is. How stupid of me!—Of course he knows—and feels for and thinks about you and all the family.

Yes—we talk about the future. We both try to keep our sense of humor. Yes—I do cry—but only when I am alone.

Some evenings, when Grandpa is too tired we play Rummy-O or cards. And I still do a little cheating—just a little.

It was so good speaking with you, the other night, and hearing about your debut into college classes. Good luck! You will be right in the swing of things very quickly.

Grandpa and I miss you so very much too. And we love you lots and lots. Keep well and Happy! More love,

Grandma

The second letter was written a little over a year after her husband died. At the time of his death, my grandmother was sixty-eight-years old, and for the first time in her life, she was alone.

Nov 20, 1981
Elana dear,

Your letter was so touching. I cried reading it. I re-read it and cried some more. There seems to be no shortage of tears, and right now the floodgates are open again.

Grandpa always worried about you "carrying the family and the world on your head and shoulders." Well—everything is going to be alright—and we have a lot to look forward to. I thank G-d for my blessings, you being a special one of them.

Must close this note before it floats to you.

I love and miss you very much!!—More love —

(Patchkey) Grams.

My grandmother used many salutations to close her letters to me: Oceans of love. Oceans and mountains of love. Mountains and oceans of love. Oodles and oodles of love. Oodles, bunches, and more love. Clusters and bunches of love. Hugs and kisses and more love. More love. Love you lots and lots. I miss you and love you very much. Keep well. Have fun. Love, love, love! I miss you all the time, everywhere!

Mothers
Over the years, I asked my grandmother questions about her mother, Ella, the woman after whom I'm named. Toward the end of her life, I got bold.

Elana: Did you get along with your mother?

Grandma: Mom (as in Mom and Pop) depended on me to go everywhere with her.

Elana: As a child or as an adult?

Grandma: Both. She was very gentle, always protecting me from my sister and brothers.

Elana: Were you ever angry at her?

Grandma: No. Not at her. I was angry at myself for letting her take over so many things.

Elana: Did you get mad? What was it like when she took over?

Grandma: She thought she was doing right by taking over. All right, we'll let it go as it is.

And that was the end of the conversation.

Over the years, I asked my mother questions about her mother, my grandmother.

"My mother was never around. She was always with her mother. I had caretakers from the time I came home from the hospital. Nurses. Then Nannies. We had Stella and Mary. My mother favored Charles, and my father favored me. It's amazing Charles and I are so close. When I was little, I was always falling off my bike and bruising my legs. The first time my mother took care of my bruises, she said, 'Okay Ann this isn't going to hurt,' and then she poured on the hydrogen peroxide, and it killed. After that, I knew I could never trust her. I could trust my father. He would say, 'Ann, this is going to hurt, but we'll blow together, and it will take the pain away'. My mother was very intrusive. She went through my drawers and she read the letters Joel (her teenage boyfriend who later became her husband and my father) wrote to me. When I was around thirteen, I knew I wasn't going to mother my children the way my mother mothered me."

Only after my grandmother's death did my mother understand her mother's relationship with me. "You were the daughter I could never be."

Truth is: I was the daughter my mother should have been, the daughter my grandmother would not let her be. I was the one who received my grandmother's unconditional love. I was the one in whom my grandmother delighted. She delighted in my writing. She delighted in my becoming a rabbi. She delighted in whatever I did. She saw me as her continuation, her completion. So much so, I became her favorite. She did it again. She repeated her favoritism in the next generation. My siblings told me, "You're Gram's favorite". My parents told me, "You're Gram's favorite. She is so obvious. All she talks about is you even when we're on a completely different topic. It's annoying."

Her favoritism toward me became a family joke. My siblings and my parents and my uncle and her caregivers teased her about it. What's most incredible is that my sister and my brother continued to visit, care for, and love her, despite her favoritism. Even more incredible: They continued to love me.

Names

My grandmother's Hebrew/Yiddish name was: *Devora Faiga*. *Devora*, from the Hebrew meaning "swarm of bees," and "to speak kind words." Both were true. When my grandmother felt taken advantage of, or when she did not trust someone, her words stung, but when she loved, she showered kindness. *Faiga*, from the Yiddish, *fayg*, meaning, "fig," or *feigel*, meaning bird. I prefer the bird interpretation. My grandmother was always ready to fly, to take off, to explore, to soar. When she was in her late eighties, I asked her if she would go skydiving.

Grandma: Sure.

Elana: Are you crazy?

Grandma: What do I have to lose?

Only later did I understand. She had outlived most of her friends, and in her mind skydiving (even if it meant death) wouldn't have been a bad way to go. It might have been better than the way she went.

My grandmother had other names: Her husband called her Dot. Her children called her Mom, Ma, or Grams. Her grandchildren called her, Grams, Grandma, Grammy, Granny, Putchkey, Buballee, and Pupalee. Aside from Hokey Pokey Grandma, her great grandchildren called her Great Grammy. Before she died, she had eight great grandchildren, and she met them all, though I doubt she remembered.

Objects

After my grandmother died, I spent three days and three nights in her condo. Those nights, I stayed awake until 2:00, and 3:00, and 4:00 a.m. rummaging through her drawers and closets and bookshelves to see what I could find.

I found underwear, slips, girdles, blouses, tee shirts, skirts, socks, dresses, Depends, robes, pantyhose, slippers, handkerchiefs, pincushions, pocketbooks, calendars, magnifying glasses, word searches, three glass-bead necklaces, a faux gold ring, faux gold earrings, fifteen Torah Fund pins, Jean Nate Moisturizing Body Wash, Sure Antiperspirant, a hairbrush whose clear bristles were filled with white hair, plastic gray-framed eye glasses with large oval lenses, beige orthopedic shoes, a Speidel 14-karat solid white-gold Hamilton hand-wound wrist watch with a broken band, a square face, and a birthday inscription on the back, "Dot, from Hy, 3-26-36," and Kodak envelopes filled with photographs of her children, grandchildren, and great grandchildren.

There was also a metal cane, a metal walker, a black foldable wheelchair, and two Medic Alert necklaces, a composite of which reads: "PACEMAKER. ARRHYTHMIA. TWO HEART VALUES REPLACED. TAKES COUMADIN, K-DUR, DIGOXIN, LASIX. ALLERGIC TO CODEINE, SULFA."

I found membership cards: The Metropolitan Museum of Art, Friends of New York Public Library, People For The American Way, Women In The Arts, League of Women Voters, Religious Coalition for Reproductive Choice, Common Cause, B'nai Brith, Women's American ORT, World Jewish Congress, The Jewish Museum, The United States Holocaust Memorial Museum, AARP Health Care Options, AARP Medicare RX Plans.

I found a newspaper clipping from 1993, with a reprint of an article from The Associated Press entitled, "How To Boost Your Self-Esteem." The article began, "The key to happiness and success is getting rid of those negative thoughts and feeling good about yourself."

I found a handful of letters my grandfather had written to my grandmother when they were courting in 1935. I read one letter, and then another, and then another, searching for love. But my grandfather's letters, while sprinkled with distant affection, spoke more of his day-to-day doings than of love.

Here is what I kept: Three pairs of my grandmother's soft pastel-colored socks, two white tee shirts, her Medic Alert Necklaces, and her wrist watch.

I wear her socks and they warm my feet.

I wear her tee shirts and I feel as if she is hugging me.

Sometimes, I don one of her Medic Alert necklaces and I remember listening to her pacemakerheart tick-tock like a clock.

On occasion, I wind her watch. It still ticks.

Pupse

After my grandmother gave birth to my mother, the obstetrician examined her in her hospital room, and she *pupsed* (her word for farted).

"Excuse me, doctor," said my grandmother.

"Don't apologize Mrs. Shanok, " the doctor said. "When I hear that sound it's a feather in my cap."

My grandmother didn't miss a beat. "Then stand at the foot of my bed, and I'll make an Indian chief out of you."

Quotes/Misquotes

Pupse. (fart).

Oh boy, oh joy, where do we go from here?

Ho, ho, ho, and a bottle of rum.

And she laughed so.

A good time was had by all.

Too much much.

Tyenol (Tylenol).

Talberts (Talbots).

Salad Nicozee (nicoise).

Heddo (hello).

Dysexic (dyslexic).

Disorientated (disoriented).

Record

In my grandmother's bookshelf, I found a record of the first fourteen years her life, penned in her own hand, in 1927, as an assignment for her English class at Flatbush. Two pieces of thick green cardboard serve as the book's cover, held together by two large metal rings. Entitled, "My Life," these ten chapters fit into forty-two lined pages filled with stories and twenty unlined pages filled with photographs. These pages have turned beige and brittle with age and they crumble like crackers.

My grandmother wrote most about her summers in Mountain Dale, New York, Fallsburgh, New York, and Lakewood, New Jersey. She rarely wrote about school. She didn't like school. She liked to be outside and she liked to swim and she liked to run free.

To my grandmother, who lived a privileged and sheltered life, the events of the day mattered little. About World War I she wrote, "The World War broke out in 1914, as we all know from history as well as hearing it from relatives and older folks. Of course, I didn't know what it was all about at that time." And why should she? She was only two-years old. But twelve years later, when she penned this account, she offered little reflection. In 1918, when she was six, her family moved to South Fourth Street, behind The Farberware factory. Her fourteen-year old accounting: "We moved because it was necessary for my father to be in the factory more often then usual on account of the war as it was very hard to get workmen." Still, little reflection.

What mattered most to my grandmother was Mrs. Walstrom's "Good and Bad Book," that was read to their father every evening. An example of one day's entry. "Monday. Isidor—very very good. Estelle—ugly at table. Milton—very bad, teased Dorothy, ugly to Estelle, fought with Isidor. Dorothy—fairly good, was cranky at table." For every very good, their father rewarded them a penny, and for every bad and very bad, their father rewarded them with "the cat-a-nine-tails."

Most intriguing to me is my grandmother's summary of her childhood illnesses: Scarlet fever in 1915, when she was three, influenza in 1918, when she was six, the measles in 1920, when she was eight, and rheumatic fever in 1921, when she was nine. Her rheumatic fever, which left her with a bad heart, she described in detail. A pain first in one leg, then in the other, causing her to limp. Pain in her joints, causing lack of mobility in her arms. A nosebleed for two nights in a row. Two months in bed, unable to sit up, and having to be fed.

When I read through this record, I love looking at the photographs. My grandmother is pictured from infant to toddler to child to young woman and she is dressed in hair ribbons, ruffled dresses, knee-highs, leotards, lace-up boots, and tank swim suits. Sometimes, she is pictured alone, other times with her siblings, parents, caretaker, governess, or friends. There is even a photograph of her family's mansion-like home on 44 Marlboro Road in Brooklyn. But I am most captivated by a photograph of my grandmother from 1925, when she was thirteen. I stare at this photograph of a curly-haired thirteen-year old many times before I realize that this young woman looks like me, not now, but years ago, when I was in college, and had a perm, and this intrigues me, because my grandmother and I didn't resemble one another in the least.

Shit

In June 2003 my grandmother came to Baltimore for the weekend of my father's retirement celebration. Too out-of-it to attend synagogue on Saturday morning, she stayed home. Three hours later when we returned for lunch, she was still in her bathrobe. Our family gathered around the dining room table: My grandmother, my parents', me, my sister, my brother, our spouses, and our children, which now number eight, but which then numbered five.

Shortly after we sat down to eat, it smelled like shit. The soles of shoes were checked. No shit. A little later, my mother spotted a pile of shit on the floor. She followed it to my grandmother.

"Grams," I said, "Let's you and me get up from the table."

My grandmother had no idea why I asked her to get up from the table, but she trusted me and as she followed me to my parents' bathroom I told her that she had an accident, that she might have poop on her, and that I would clean her up.

I helped her sit on the toilet. She seemed unaware that shit had seeped out of her, that she smelled like shit, that she had shit all over her clothes, her slippers, her tush, and her legs. I asked her to lean forward. I wiped away the crusted poop from the top of her tush and I wiped the looser poop from her lower tush and I wiped her tush. I wiped her thighs. I wiped her legs. I removed her pink terry cloth slippers. I wiped her feet. I removed her floral robe and nightgown and I placed them in the sink to soak. I cleaned her pink terry cloth slippers. I cleaned the yellow floor tiles. I helped my grandmother into her Depends. I dressed her in a beige skirt and a white short-sleeve cotton shirt and I placed white terry cloth slippers on her feet and I ushered her back to her seat at the table and I pushed her in, as if she were a toddler. Then, I walked into the kitchen and I cried.

TMI: Too Much Information

A few years after my grandfather died, my mother, my sister and I helped my grandmother downsize from her Scarsdale home to a New Rochelle condo. We spent a few days in her attic opening one cardboard box after another, searching for treasures to keep. In one cardboard box, I discovered an antique satin maroon robe that, from waist to neck, hosted fifty satin Chinese knot buttons. "Grams, this is gorgeous. Can I have it?" I asked. "Sure," she said. She smiled, and stared into the distance. I began to unhook the fifty loops from the knot buttons around which they were fastened, and found myself mumbling in frustration, "This is ridiculous. These things don't open." My grandmother laughed. "That's what Grandpa used to say."

Some years later, when Sarina and I helped my grandmother dress for a Passover Seder, my grandmother said, with a girlish giggle and a sparkle in her hazel eyes, "I was much more sexually experimental than your grandfather."

Undying

Her smell: Channel # 5.

Her recipe for rosy cheeks: Dab each cheek with two lipstick dots and rub.

Her ability to apply a perfect coat of lipstick without a mirror.

Her love of flea markets. Cheap watches. Word searches.

Her camp memories: skinny dipping in the lake, and sneaking frogs into her counselor's bed.

Serving Sarina and I (her pre-teen granddaughters) a nightcap of Mint Julep with water and lots of ice.

Stopping during walks, because she was too tired to continue, and rather than admit her exhaustion, she would pretend she had stopped to tell a story about the school, or apartment building, or stop sign, or tree near where she stood.

Helping us, her four grandchildren, find the Passover *afikoman* that she and my grandfather had hidden.

Running to the toilet with her skirt half-up and her girdle half-down.

Walking around her house or condo naked.

Requesting warm rolls at restaurants, and when the waitress would say no, her response, "What's wrong you don't have an oven here?"

Walking into the bathroom when I was showering, opening the shower curtain to see if I had enough soap and shampoo, watching me shower for a moment or two, and commenting on how my body was developing.

Driving Teresa, her New Rochelle housekeeper, into Manhattan to scrub the gray and grimy shower stall in my rabbinical school dorm.

Telling her I wanted to move to California to begin rabbinical school instead of remaining in Manhattan, closer to her, and her words, "You must listen to your heart."

Coming to Park Avenue Synagogue where I served as a rabbi for five years to hear me speak, and telling me how she had turned to the people sitting next to her, and asked what they thought of their woman rabbi, without letting on that she was the rabbi's grandmother.

Being the first family member to meet Seth, the man I would marry.

Dead in a plain pine box.

Venice

In June 1985, when I was twenty-four and Sarina was twenty-one, and our grandmother was seventy-four, she treated us to a vacation in Rome and Venice, a vacation similar to one she and my grandfather had taken in 1961. We stayed in the same hotels: In Rome, at the Excelsior Hotel, and in Venice, at Hotel Danieli. We visited the same sites: The Palace Museum, Tivoli Gardens, and the Venice Ghetto.

My grandmother's journal, a four-by-six-inch yellow spiral notebook, described the details of our trip from the people we met to the placemats we purchased to the sites we saw to the guides we toured with to the restaurants we frequented.

"Checked into Excelsior looked same as it did in 1961—painted since then—our room was nice."

"Elana and Sarina writing letters—I trying to remember all that happened."

Her thoughts on two nights before we fell asleep, "Giggled—laughed until exhausted." Girls "were up so late talking, laughing, and enjoying being together it was wonderful."

About Ville d'Este Gardens, "Gardens not kept the way I remember them 25 years ago with Hy."

About our tour to the Vatican Museum, Library Hall and the Sistine Chapel, "Tour guide—awful—voice and canned speech and not nice."

About the Peggy Guggenheim Museum which she visited on her own, "People viewing were more interesting than paintings. Gardens had grave of Peggy and all her dogs—with names and dates of births and deaths of about 15 of them. Told the girls about it—they said 'How Gross'—the way I felt too. Oh well, we're all crazy in different ways I guess."

About the Spanish synagogue in the Venice Ghetto that was closed for repairs, "That is the one Hy and I went into."

About our time in Venice, "Had dinner in hotel. It was very good—should be for price it cost. Ate and ate—too much much. Went for a little walk—girls a riot wanted to carry me. Fun—fun!"

About our parting at the Leonardo da Vinci airport in Rome, "They walked me to my gate—saw me off—then they went to their gate. Boarding plane found two seats next to me vacant. Maybe they too felt girls should be going back with me."

Wisdom

About turning store-bought into homemade. Sprinkle cinnamon into Mott's Applesauce. Add extra milk and fresh mushrooms to Campbell's Cream of Mushroom Soup.

About dating: Always keep the door open.

About one particular man: Honey, you're smarter than he is. Don't let him know. Let him think he's smarter. A man needs to feel this way.

About showering: Always end with cold water. Closes the pores.

About vaginas: Don't wear underwear to bed. Your vagina needs to breathe.

About bras: You need good support.

About family, even distant family, even annoying family: Family is family. Always call and get together.

About how to cheat when playing Solitaire: When you can't make any more moves, slip the card on top of the deck to the bottom of the deck, and begin again.

About cheating at Solitaire: It's not cheating if you're playing against yourself.

About prayer: Don't *nudgy* God too much.

About life: Have fun. Relax. Don't take things too seriously.

Xenia

My grandmother loved to buy us gifts, especially clothes. It gave her great pleasure to take us, her four grandchildren, clothes' shopping before Rosh Hashanah and Passover. Her favorite stores: Saks Fifth Avenue, Lord and Taylor, Bloomingdales, Macys, and Alexander's. She loved searching the racks and bringing skirts, blouses, dresses, and sweaters into the dressing room for Sarina and me to try on, and suits, slacks, shirts, and ties for Rafi and Ari to try on. Some of her choices we were less than thrilled about and we let her know. Grandma, I'm not putting that on. It makes me look like a penguin, or like I should be on an episode of Little House on the Prairie, or like I'm living on a shtetl in Poland. Sometimes, she would be annoyed, other times, she would laugh, but she would always make us try on the despised article of clothing.

Our holiday shopping sprees worked like this. For three days we shopped. For three evenings we put on fashion shows for my grandfather and my parents (if they were there). To the best of my memory, we hated these fashion shows, but my grandmother loved them. She loved them because she delighted seeing all we had accomplished and she loved them because she delighted in all the praise she received for her day's work.

During college, graduate school, and even after I entered the rabbinate, I continued to shop for clothes with my grandmother. "What do we need to accomplish?" she'd ask. "Make a list. Do you need dress shoes, sneakers, socks, bras, underwear, pajamas, slacks, tops, skirts, dresses, or bathing suits? Just put it all down so we don't forget anything."

Year: 1912

The year of 1912 was the year New Mexico became the forty-seventh state in the union, the year Arizona became the forty-eighth state in the union, the year the Titanic sank, the year Woodrow Wilson was elected president, the year the South African Native National Congress was established, the year the Girl Scouts of America was founded, the year Tiger Stadium opened in Detroit, the year Fenway Park opened in Boston, the year the suffragettes and their supporters paraded in New

York City, the year the Columbia University School of Journalism opened, the year of the first motorized movie camera, the year of the Dixie Cup, the year the first Japanese Cherry Blossoms were planted in Washington D.C., the year China became a Republic, the year of the first Balkan war, the year Albania announced independence from the Ottoman Empire, the year a fire in Constantinople destroyed 1,120 buildings, the year sodomy became legal in France, and the year the Polish biochemist Casimir Funk created the category of medication known as vitamins. But most important to me: 1912 was the year my grandmother was born.

Zoetic: Pertaining to Life, Living, Vital
I recently created a collage of photographs from the last few decades in my grandmother's life. The collage sits in my office on my file cabinet waiting for a home inside a fitting frame I have yet to find. We keep an eye on each other, my grandmother and I. She smiles at me, and I smile back. I imagine her childlike spirit and I frolic forward.

Bracelet

Sarah Stickney

You had a string bracelet on your wrist,
and I wanted it off;
that's what my love is like—
it wants you naked of everything. you've learned
or acquired, every last mechanism shed.
It wants you like a crime scene, wiped clean
of fingerprints by the thieves.

The Hopes

You get everything you want, just
at the wrong time, like diagonal
rain on a Tuesday morning, after
your lover sucked a bruise big
as a bougainvillea in the cradle
between shoulder and neck. Although
you were sweetly convulsing, cold
crept up around your ribs. You
are exquisitely small and unimportant
is what you will tell yourself
when you get home, hoping
to grow up. Hoping to grow thin
you will eat nervously and often.
You will place the daffodils
on your kitchen table in the hopes
that so rarely have an object, or
not a real one, anyway.

From the Very Start

Paulann Petersen

—for William Stafford, whose first word was moon

The first word your tongue formed
for another's ear
was full as a lighted globe
travelling the dark. Maybe someone
tried to hear you say *Mama*,
but what you uttered was so deep
at its two-fold center,
the roundness of its saying
left no room for doubt.

A room inside this sound
opened without wall or ceiling,
a passage wide as what your eyes
could take in, thin as a single
gold thread leading you through
each word-swept day. In the sky,
night or day, a glimpse of what
first shaped your breath

still sweeps my breath away—
a ready gleam that's constant
only in endless surprise.

Seeker

A rose-apple branch gripped in her hand,
Nandutta walked, debating religion with anyone
who challenged her, converting to Buddha
once she found her equal, a man, a speaker of Buddhist truth.
I could too. I could wander my neighborhood
like Nandutta wandered hers
in India, long ago—yes I could.
If I knew enough to debate
with someone, knew what *rose-apple* is. And I don't.
Maybe flowering quince would do.

So I back my car out
from beside the house onto the street.
This winter morning rain-smeared, dark,
the car windows fogged. I look up and down the cross-street.
Careful, slow. Then starting to go, hit the brakes,
stop short. Right in front of me, a man is crossing the street,
corner to corner. He veers and approaches my car.
From under an umbrella, his bearded face peers
into the window I roll down.
He says yesterday riding his bike he was hit,

someone hit him with her car. A woman about my age.
Oh dear, I say, and you're thinking it was me?
that one from yesterday? I don't say aloud,
but think *I've never seen you before,*
I didn't even come close.
He smiles. Says no, he's just
telling me a true story.

Blossoms, then leaves, fell off my quince bush months ago.
Its still-clinging fruits—like small, wizened apples—
Now gleam in plain view.
I'm old. I know precious little
about the Buddha. There's nothing
but a steering wheel in my hand's grip.
Close enough. I've met my match.

Nine Symbols

—on my 70th birthday

The garden I planted. The one I didn't
now filled with a plant's seeding itself into spots
I saved for something else. A once sought-after
bulb's blastula bent on claiming
all available space.

My house still handsome but crumbling—
wavering glass of its Victorian windows
arced with light-catching cracks.
Wallpaper lifting away in unmoored swatches.
A fine, big, hand-knotted rug
hiding my floor's blistered varnish.

That make-over that money could buy?
A much too expensive patch-up.

Good-as-new? A lure that's now at least
half a century gone.

In the World Lying Worlds Below

To eat a morsel of the underworld's dream-food
is to die a bit. So *that's* what I've been doing
each night in my dream-life: eating
and dying, eating and dying. No.
Not so. I don't recall a dream when I actually *ate*.
One when I fried wolf meat
in a cast iron skillet, yes. And dreams where
wedding cakes lifted their tiers
like storyed building
white in the sun. But none where I sat
moving food from platter to plate,
balancing forkfuls into my mouth.

But wait. Foolish me—
to be busy thinking up ways
I might remember my way out of death.
No doubt a spatter from that searing wildness
found the lips I licked. Surely I slipped
a crumb of that dream-cake under my tongue.

In Motion

No. I don't know how a story works—
How tyrannies of time and space
reclaim the tailings, heap by heap,
of pretense and memory, how the narrative
seems to plead for a little violence,
a sharp edge swung against flesh,
and at the end, the story's bruise
rising to show its color.

To create character is, for me,
a process of complete mystery.
To make a *he* talk through lips of described
color and shape demands that a *she*
answer, commanding a plot
of alternate sympathies, a need
to tinker with verbs, to avoid
what simply *is*. A story's sentences
could then haggle for given proportion,
even set up housekeeping rules,
a strict division of labor.

I choose the alternative any day,
every day—a little aimless ramble
over fresh grass, my footprints
springing into disappearance behind me,
motion's sake making my way
into the poem's wild blank yonder.
Come what may.

Contributors

Erin Bealmear's poetry has been published in *The Cortland Review*, *Painted Bride Quarterly*, *Blip*, *Margie*, *XConnect*, *The Santa Clara Review*, *Opium*, and *Main Street Rag*, among others. She was also awarded a *South Carolina Review* poetry award and was a finalist for the New Issues Poetry Prize.

Kevin Boyle's book, *A Home for Wayward Girls*, was published by New Issues, and his poems have appeared or are forthcoming in *Alaska Quarterly*, *Fourth River*, *Hollins Critic*, *Poetry East*, *Pleiades*, and *Virginia Quarterly Review*. Originally from Philadelphia, Kevin teaches at Elon University in North Carolina.

Noel Conneely has had work in *Coe Review*, *Chelsea*, *Main Street Rag*, *Willow Review*, *Yellow Medicine Review*, and other publications in Ireland, Great Britain and the U.S.A. He has taught Irish in Dunlavin for many years. He is seeking a publisher for a first collection.

Robert Cooperman is the author of 14 poetry collections, most recently *Little Timothy in Heaven* (March Street Press) and *The Lily of the West* (Wind Publications). *In the Colorado Gold Fever Mountains* won the Colorado Book Award in 2000. Cooperman won the Holland Prize from Logan House Books, with *My Shtetl*. His work has appeared in *The Sewanee Review*, *The North American Review*, *California Quarterly*, and previously in *CLR*.

Holly Day is a housewife and mother of two living in Minneapolis, Minnesota, who teaches needlepoint classes in the Minneapolis school district. Her poetry has recently appeared in *The Worcester Review*, *Broken Pencil*, and *Slipstream*, and she is the recipient of the 2011 Sam Ragan Poetry Prize from Barton College. Her most recent published book is *Notenlesen für Dummies Das Pocketbuch*, while her novel, *The Trouble With Clare*, is due out from Hydra Publications in 2013.

Darrell Dela Cruz graduated from San Jose State's MFA Program for Poetry. His works have been published in *Thin Air, Third Wednesday,* and *ZAUM*, and will appear forthcoming in *Two-Thirds North*. He tries to analyze a poem a day on his blog http://retailmfa.blogspot.com/ or rather he acknowledges his misinterpretations of poems for all the internet to read.

Christine DeSimone is a fourth-generation Californian who practices law in San Francisco. Her poems have appeared in *Alaska Quarterly Review, Cream City Review, Zyzzyva*, and many other journals. Her first full-length collection, *How Long the Night Is*, is forthcoming from Lummox Press in late 2013.

2013 marks **Brian C. Felder's** 44th year on the American poetry scene, a career that has seen 250 of his poems published in 106 different print magazines across the US. This, however, is Felder's first appearance in *CLR* and he couldn't be happier to share his work with a new audience of readers.

Anthony Fife lives in Yellow Springs, Ohio, with his partner, fiction writer Lauren Shows, and their daughter Lucy. Anthony accepted his

B.A. and M.A. in English from Morehead State University and his M.F.A in Poetry from Spalding University. Anthony teaches English at Clark State Community College and Sinclair Community College, and is the founder of the Yellow Springs Reading Series.

James Grabill's recent work has appeared in numerous periodicals such as the *Buddhist Poetry Review* (US), *The Oxonian Review* (UK), *Stand* (UK), *Magma* (UK), *Toronto Quarterly* (CAN), *Harvard Review* (US), *Terrain* (US), *Seneca Review* (US), *Weber*, and others. His books include *An Indigo Scent after the Rain* and *Poem Rising Out of the Earth*. Wordcraft of Oregon will publish his new project of environmental prose poems, *Sea-Level Nerve: Book I* this summer, and *Book II* next summer. He teaches "systems thinking" relative to sustainability.

Carl W. Graham is a custodian at Clackamas Community College where he not only cleans the classrooms but often has the privilege of attending classes in them as well. He loves funny hats, old monster movies, his wife Sharman, and stories that are well told.

Twice-nominated for the Pushcart Prize, **Jonathan Greenhause** was a runner-up in the 2012 *Georgetown Review* Prize and is the author of a chapbook, *Sebastian's Relativity* (Anobium Books). In addition to previously appearing in *CLR*, his poems have been published or are forthcoming in *Hawai'i Pacific Review*, *Midwest Quarterly Review*, *New Delta Review*, *Popshot* (UK), and *Regime* (AUS), among others.

John Grey is an Australian born poet, playwright, musician, and Providence, RI, resident since the late seventies. He works as a financial systems analyst. He has been published in numerous magazines, including *Weird Tales*, *Christian Science Monitor*, *Agni*, *Poet Lore*, and *Journal Of The American Medical Association*, as well as the horror anthology *What Fears Become*, with work upcoming in *Sanskrit*, *GW Review*, and the *Potomac Review*. John has had plays produced in Los Angeles and off-off Broadway in New York. He was the winner of the Rhysling Award for short genre poetry in 1999.

Patrick Hicks is the author of five poetry collections, most recently *Finding the Gossamer* and *This London*—he is also the editor of *A Harvest of Words*, which was funded by the National Endowment for the Humanities. His work has appeared in some of the most vital literary magazines in America, including *Ploughshares*, *Glimmer Train*, *The Missouri Review*, *Tar River Poetry*, *New Ohio Review*, *Salon*, and many others. He has been nominated seven times for the Pushcart Prize, he has been a finalist for the High Plains Book Award, the Dzanc Books Short Story Collection Competition, and the Gival Press Novel Award. He has earned notable mentions in *Best American Stories* and he has won the *Glimmer Train* Fiction Award, as well as a number of grants, including one from the Bush Artist Foundation. He is the Writer-in-Residence at Augustana College and, during summer months, you'll usually find him in Ireland.

As founding editor of Many Voices Press, **Lowell Jaeger** compiled *Poems Across the Big Sky*, an anthology of Montana poets, and *New Poets of the American West*, an anthology of poets from 11 Western states. His third collection of poems, *Suddenly Out of a Long Sleep* (Arctos Press) was published in 2009 and was a finalist for the Paterson Award. His fourth collection, *WE*, (Main Street Rag Press) was published in 2010. He is the recipient of fellowships from the National Endowment for the Arts and the Montana Arts Council and winner of the Grolier Poetry Peace Prize. Most recently Jaeger was awarded the Montana Governor's Humanities Award for his work in promoting thoughtful civic discourse.

William Jolliff serves as professor of English at George Fox University. His chapbook, *Whatever Was Ripe*, won the 1997 Bright Hill Press poetry competition; and his edited collection, *The Poetry of John Greenleaf Whittier: A Readers' Edition*, was published by Friends United Press. Bill has published critical articles and poems in over a hundred periodicals, including *Northwest Review*, *Southern Humanities Review*, *Midwest Quarterly*, *Christianity and Literature*, and *Appalachian Journal*. His most recent chapbook is *Searching for a White Crow* (2009).

Shane Kash is a manufacturing student at Clackamas Community College intending to work in the fast-paced world of CNC machining. He spent a total of five months "on the ice" over the 2010-11 science season at McMurdo Station, Antarctica. Though a native of Michigan, he resides in NE Portland with his wife and one-year-old son.

John P. Kristofco is a professor of English and former dean at the University of Akron. His poetry and short stories have appeared in over a hundred different publications, including *Folio*, *Cimarron Review*, *Poem*, *The Cape Rock*, *Illya's Honey*, *Caveat Lector*, *Small Pond*, *The Aurorean*, *Bitterroot*, *Rattle*, *Iodine*, *The Rockhurst Review*, *The Bryant Literary Review*, and *California Quarterly*. He has published two chapbooks, *A Box of Stones* and *Apparitions*, and has been nominated for the Pushcart Prize five times.

Ted Lardner's work has appeared in *5am*, *Arsenic Lobster*, *The Normal School*, and other journals. Tornado, published in 2008, was the winner of the Wick Poetry Center's chapbook competition. A yoga teacher and professor of English, he lives in Ohio with his family.

Jessica Lilien has work published or forthcoming in *LUMINA Journal*, *Columbia: A Journal of Literature and Art Online*, *Morpheus Tales Magazine*, the anthology *Night Terrors III*, and *TRIVIA: Voices of Feminism*. Her short story "After Saco River" was one of the winners of the LUMINA XII 2013 Fiction Contest, judged by George Saunders. He called it "very strange." She lives in Brooklyn.

T Jay McCollum is a student at Clackamas Community College.

John McKernan, who grew up in Omaha, Nebraska, is now a retired Comma Herder/Phonics Coach after teaching 41 years at Marshall University. He lives, mostly, in West Virginia, where he edits ABZ Press. His most recent book of selected poems is *Resurrection of the Dust*. He has published poems in *The Atlantic Monthly*, *The Paris Review*, *The New Yorker*, *Virginia Quarterly Review*, and many other magazines.

James B. Nicola has had over 300 poems published in periodicals including *CLR* (twice before), *Atlanta Review*, *Tar River*, *Texas Review*, *Lyric*, and *Nimrod*. A Yale grad and stage director by profession, his book *Playing the Audience* won a *Choice* Award. As a poet, he also won the Dana Literary Award and a People's Choice award (from *Storyteller*); was nominated for a Pushcart Prize and a Rhysling Award; and was featured poet at *New Formalist*. His children's musical

Chimes: A Christmas Vaudeville premiered in Fairbanks, Alaska—with Santa Claus in attendance opening night.

Olivia Parkes was born in London and grew up in Southern California. She received a BA with Honors in Art History and Studio Art from Wesleyan University in 2011, and currently lives and works as an artist in Berlin.

Bri'Anne Parkin is a graduate of Clackamas Community College, where she earned her AAOT. She is currently attending Marylhurst University, and will soon finish her BFA. Bri'Anne's love for the fine arts has developed through years of experience and has shown itself through her various works. She has used photography and painting, in particular, as ways in which she can capture the natural beauties of this world that she believes are far too often overlooked. Despite her passion for art, Bri'Anne's heart lies in helping the children she loves so dearly through her work in Uganda, Africa. She plans to combine her artistic skills and training in art therapy counseling to provide long term healing for the orphans of Uganda when she moves there after finishing her degree.

Richard King Perkins II is a state-sponsored advocate for residents in long-term care facilities. He has a wife, Vickie, and a daughter, Sage. He is a three-time Pushcart nominee whose work has appeared in hundreds of publications including *Poetry Salzburg Review*, *Bluestem*, *Sheepshead Review*, *Sierra Nevada Review*, *Two Thirds North*, *The Red Cedar Review*, and *The William and Mary Review*. He has poems forthcoming in *Broad River Review*, *Emrys Journal*, *December Magazine*, and *The Louisiana Review*.

Paulann Petersen was a Stegner Fellow at Stanford and—in addition to having appeared in *CLR*—her work has been in *Poetry*, *The New Republic*, *Prairie Schooner*, *Poetry Northwest*, *Yellow Silk*, and *Willow Springs*. Paulann is currently Oregon Poet Laureate, and her most recent book of poems is *The Voluptuary*, from Lost Horse Press.

Michael D. Riley's most recent book, *Players*, a collection of narrative and character-driven poems, appeared in 2008. *Green Hills: Memoir Poems* has been accepted by Finishing Line Press. He has poems in two recent anthologies, *Irish American Poetry From the Eighteenth Century to the Present* and *Blood to Remember: American Poets on the Holocaust*. His poems have appeared in many periodicals, including *Poetry*, *Poetry Ireland Review*, *South Carolina Review*, *Cumberland Poetry Review*, *The Fiddlehead*, *Arizona Quarterly*, and *Southern Humanities Review*. He is Emeritus Professor of English from Penn State University and lives in Lancaster, PA.

Matt Schumacher, hard-working part-time English instructor at CCC, has published two collections of poetry, *Spilling the Moon* and *The Fire Diaries*, and serves as poetry editor for the New Fabulist journal, *Phantom Drift*. His poems have appeared recently in *Green Mountains Review's 25th Anniversary Issue*, *The Fiddlehead*, and *The Oregonian*.

Ire'ne Lara Silva lives in Austin, TX, and is the author of *Furia* (poetry, Mouthfeel Press, 2010) which received an Honorable Mention for the 2011 International Latino Book Award and *Flesh to Bone* (short stories, Aunt Lute Books, 2013) which won this year's Premio Aztlan, placed 2nd for the 2014 NACCS Tejas Foco Award for Fiction, and has been shortlisted for Foreward Review's Book of the Year Award in Multicultural Fiction. Ire'ne was the Fiction Finalist for ARO-HO's 2013 Gift of Freedom Award, the 2008 recipient of the Gloria Anzaldua Milagro Award, a Macondo Workshop member, and a Can-toMundo Inaugural Fellow. She and Moises S. L. Lara are currently co-coordinators for the Flor De Nopal Literary Festival.

Jeanine Stevens was raised in Indiana and has graduate degrees in An-thropology and Education. Her work has or will appear in *Tipton Poetry Review, Poesy, Alehouse, The North Dakota Review, Pearl, Verse Wisconsin, Evansville Review, Westwind,* and *Poet Lore* among others. Cherry Grove Collections published her first book, *Sailing on Milkweed* in 2012, and her latest chapbook, *Women in Cafés,* was released by Finishing Line Press. She is the recipient of poetry prizes from the Bay Area Poets Coalition, Mendocino Coast Writer's Confer-ence, Stockton Arts Commission, and Ekphrasis. Jeanine is a member of the Squaw Valley Community of Writers.

Upon earning her MFA from the University of New Hampshire, **Sarah Stickney** received a Fulbright Grant for the translation of poetry in Bologna, Italy. Her collaboration with translator Diana Thow on the selected work of Italian poet Elisa Biagini was published by Chelsea Editions under the title *The Guest in the Wood* in October 2013. Her own poems have appeared or are forthcoming in publications such as *Rhino, The Portland Review,* and *Cold Mountain Review,* among others. She teaches at St. John's College in Annapolis, MD.

Jane Stuart writes poetry, working now on cinquains and tanka, in Kentucky. Hew work has appeared in *Shemom, Edizioni Universum's*

International Poetry, Aasra, Pegasus, Write On!! Poetry Magazine, AWEN (England), and *Harp-Strings Poetry Journal.*

Nicole Taylor has many hopeful projects, a variety of styles, and a wide range of subjects. She is an artist, a hiker, a poetry notetaker, a sketcher, a volunteer, and a dancer, formerly in Salem, Oregon's, DanceAbility. Her work has been accepted by *A Handful of Stones, Four and Twenty Journal, Boneshaker: A Bicycling Almanac, Camel Saloon, Denali Literary Journal, Groundwaters Magazine, Pemmican, Queen Bee Collective*—a Eugene, Oregon online nature journal, *Red Fez, Tiger's Eye,* and msany others. She blogs at apoetessanthology.blogspot.com/ and facebook.com/ntaylortoo.

John Walser is an associate professor of English at Marian University in Fond du Lac, Wisconsin, where he teaches a wide variety of courses in literature, composition, and creative writing. He holds a doctorate in English and Creative Writing from the University of Wisconsin-Milwaukee. In 2004, along with four other poets from Fond du Lac, he co-founded the Foot of the Lake Poetry Collective, an organization that sponsors monthly poetry readings, conducts occasional workshops, and provides other opportunities to share poetry. His works has appeared or is forthcoming in a number of journals, including *Barrow Street, Nimrod, The Evansville Review, The Baltimore Review, The Monongahela Review, Verse Wisconsin* and *The Packinghouse Review.* He is currently working on three manuscripts of poems.

Leesha White has been a lover of the written word since childhood. She has a passion for the whimsy of the old writers and a love for teaching it. She lives in Clackamas, Oregon. Her hobbies include hiking, camping, fishing, and a never ceasing pursuit of the ultimate story.

John Sibley Williams is the author of *Controlled Hallucinations* (forthcoming, FutureCycle Press) and six poetry chapbooks, as well as the editor of the forthcoming *Motionless from the Iron Bridge: A Northwest Bridge Poem Anthology*. He is the winner of the HEART Poetry Award, and finalist for the Pushcart, Rumi, and The Pinch Poetry Prizes. John serves as editor of *The Inflectionist Review*, co-director of the Walt Whitman 150 project, and Marketing Director at Inkwater Press. He holds an MFA in Creative Writing and MA in Book Publishing. A few previous publishing credits include: *Third Coast, Inkwell, Bryant Literary Review, Cream City Review, The Chaffin Journal, The Evansville Review, RHINO*, and various anthologies. He lives in Portland, Oregon.

K. A. Wisniewski is the author of two artist books and editor of the anthology *The Comedy of Dave Chappelle: Critical Essays*. His creative work has most recently appeared in *basalt, The Chariton Review, MAYDAY Magazine, The Chiron Review, Bluestem, Third Wednesday*, and *CAIRN*. He is currently a Ph.D. candidate in Language, Literacy and Culture at the University of Maryland, Baltimore County.

Jeffrey Zable is a teacher and percussionist who plays Afro-Cuban folkloric music for dance classes and Rumbas around the San Francisco Bay Area. He's published five chapbooks including *Zable's Fables* with an introduction by the late great Beat poet Harold Norse. Present or upcoming work in *Toad Suck Review, Clarion, Serving House Journal, Talking River, Skidrow Penthouse, The Alarmist, Edge, Futures Trading, Owen Wister Review*, and many others.

Elana Zaiman is a rabbi, chaplain, and writer of essays, nonfictions, fictions, and articles. Her publications in literary journals include: *The Gettysburg Review*, *The Sun*, *Post Road*, *The Dalhousie Review*, *American Letters & Commentary*, *The Raven Chronicles*, *Under The Sun*, *The Beloit Fiction Journal*, *Pilgrimage*, and others.

Visit

CLACKAMAS LITERARY REVIEW

clackamasliteraryreview.org
facebook.com/clackamasliteraryreview

Contact
clr@clackamas.edu

CLACKAMAS LITERARY REVIEW

the finest writing for the best readers

Clackamas Literary Review has been committed to bringing you the best writing from around the world since 1997. Subscribe now to receive the latest and forthcoming issues.

Clackamas Literary Review

_____	1 year	$10
_____	2 years	$18
_____	3 years	$26

Name _____

Address _____

City / State / Zip _____

Email _____

Send this form and check or money order to:

Clackamas Literary Review
English Department
Clackamas Community College
19600 Molalla Avenue
Oregon City, Oregon 97045